ATLAS POETICA

A Journal of World Tanka

Number 22

M. Kei, editor
toki, editorial assistant

2015
Keibooks, Perryville, Maryland, USA

KEIBOOKS
P O Box 516
Perryville, Maryland, USA 21903
http://AtlasPoetica.org   Editor@AtlasPoetica.org

Atlas Poetica
A Journal of World Tanka

Copyright © 2015 by Keibooks

All rights reserved. No part of this book may be reproduced in any form or by any electronic or mechanical means including information storage and retrieval systems without permission in writing from the publisher, except by reviewers and scholars who may quote brief passages. See our EDUCATIONAL USE NOTICE.

Atlas Poetica : A Journal of World Tanka, an organic print and e-journal published at least three times a year. Atlas Poetica is dedicated to publishing and promoting world tanka literature, including tanka, kyoka, gogyoshi, tanka prose, tanka sequences, shaped tanka, sedoka, mondo, cherita, zuihitsu, and other variations and innovations in the field of tanka. We do not publish haiku, except as incidental to a tanka collage or other mixed form work.

Atlas Poetica is interested in all verse of high quality, but our preference is for tanka literature that is authentic to the environment and experience of the poet. While we will consider tanka in the classical Japanese style, our preference is for fresh, forward-looking tanka that engages with the world as it is. We are willing to consider experiments and explorations as well as traditional approaches.

In addition to verse, *Atlas Poetica* publishes articles, essays, reviews, interviews, letters to the editor, etc., related to tanka literature. Tanka in translation from around the world are welcome in the journal.

Published by Keibooks

ISBN 978-1514832493 (Print)
AtlasPoetica.org

TABLE OF CONTENTS

Editorial
Educational Use Notice........................4
Ryuka and the Expanding World of
Tanka Literature, M. Kei 5

Poets
Alexis Rotella 7
Allistair Wilson 7
Andrew Howe 10, 11, 56
Andy McCall 11
Autumn Noelle Hall 12, 13, 14
Bill Waters 16
Bruce England............................17
Carole Johnston..........................18
Chen-ou Liu 20, 21
Dave Read 22
David Klasovsky 23
Debbie Strange...........................25
Don Miller 14
Elizabeth Howard 26, 27
Gerry Jacobson..........................28, 29
Grunge 27
Janet Butler............................29
Janet Lynn Davis 30
Jonathan Vos Post.........................31
Joy McCall...31, 32, 33, 34, 35, 36, 37, 38,
44, 45, 67, 73
Kayla Daley 38
Kath Abela Wilson 39
Ken Slaughter 40
Larry Kimmel 41, 42
Liam Wilkinson 43, 44, 45, 75
M. Kei 5, 51, 52, 79
Maggie Gladding 53
Marilyn Humbert.......................54, 55, 56
Marilyn Morgan.........................57
Marsha Oseas............................58, 59, 60
Marshall Bood............................60
Matsukaze 61, 64
Mira N. Mataric 65
Murasame 64
Patricia Prime.....77, 88, 90, 92, 94, 95, 97
Peter Fiore 65, 66

Rebecca Drouilhet 66
Robert Epstein..........................67
Ryoh Honda 67, 74
Sanford Goldstein.......................69
Sandi Pray 70
Susan Burch 71
Susan King 72
Tim Callahan 73
Tony Beyer 73
Vyonne McLelland-Howe 11, 73
Yiwei Huang 39

Articles
A Note about Ryuka, Ryoh Honda 74
*Weaponness : Climbing Towards an
Understanding of Ryūka, Essay and Ryūka*,
Liam Wilkinson 75
The Explosion of Tanka, Patricia
Prime................................77
*Substructure in Tanka : the Strophe, Line, and
Poetic Phrase*, M. Kei 79
Review: *Journeys: Getting Lost*, by Carole
Johnston, Reviewed by Patricia
Prime................................88
Review: *Dancing With Another Me*, by
Gerry Jacobson, Reviewed by Patricia
Prime................................90
Review: *This Tanka Whirl*, by Sanford
Goldstein, Reviewed by Patricia
Prime................................92
Review: *All You Need Is Love*, edited by
Amelia Fielden, Reviewed by Patricia
Prime................................94
Review: *Gusts No. 21*, edited by Kozue
Uzawa, Reviewed by Patricia
Prime................................95
Review: *From the Middle Country : The
Third Tanka Collection* by Noriko
Tanaka, Reviewed by Patricia Prime
................................97

Announcements................................100

Educational Use Notice

Keibooks of Perryville, Maryland, USA, publisher of the journal, *Atlas Poetica : A Journal of World Tanka*, is dedicated to tanka education in schools and colleges, at every level. It is our intention and our policy to facilitate the use of *Atlas Poetica* and related materials to the maximum extent feasible by educators at every level of school and university studies.

Educators, without individually seeking permission from the publisher, may use *Atlas Poetica : A Journal of World Tanka's* online digital editions and print editions as primary or ancillary teaching resources. Copyright law "Fair Use" guidelines and doctrine should be interpreted very liberally with respect to *Atlas Poetica* precisely on the basis of our explicitly stated intention herein. This statement may be cited as an effective permission to use *Atlas Poetica* as a text or resource for studies. Proper attribution of any excerpt to *Atlas Poetica* is required. This statement applies equally to digital resources and print copies of the journal.

Individual copyrights of poets, authors, artists, etc., published in *Atlas Poetica* are their own property and are not meant to be compromised in any way by the journal's liberal policy on "Fair Use." Any educator seeking clarification of our policy for a particular use may email the Editor of *Atlas Poetica* at editor@AtlasPoetica.org. We welcome innovative uses of our resources for tanka education.

Atlas Poetica
Keibooks
P O Box 516
Perryville, MD 21903
<http://AtlasPoetica.org>

Editorial Biographies

M. Kei is the editor of *Atlas Poetica* and editor-in-chief of *Take Five : Best Contemporary Tanka*. He is a tall ship sailor in real life and has published nautical novels featuring a gay protagonist, *Pirates of the Narrow Seas*. His most recent novel is an Asian-themed science fiction/fantasy novel, *Fire Dragon*.

toki is a published poet and editorial assistant for Keibooks. Born and raised in the Pacific Northwest US, toki often writes poetry informed by the experience of that region: the labyrinthine confines of the evergreen forests, the infinite vastness of the sea and inclement sky, and the liminal spaces in between. toki's poetry can be found online and in print, with work published in *Atlas Poetica*, *The Bamboo Hut*, and *Poetry Nook*.

Our 'butterfly' is actually an Atlas moth (Attacus atlas), the largest butterfly/moth in the world. It comes from the tropical regions of Asia. Image from the 1921 *Les insectes agricoles d'époque*.

Ryuka and the Expanding World of Tanka Literature

In this issue we have a focus on ryuka, the Okinawan form related to tanka. A four line poem in the pattern of 8-8-8-6 syllables, the thirty syllables of ryuka are similar to tanka in length. This has led some to describe it as the "Okinawan form of tanka," but the structure is quite different. We are fortunate to have not one, but two articles on ryuka from different perspectives, along with classical and contemporary ryuka by Ryoh Honda, Matsukaze, and Liam Wilkinson. *Atlas Poetica* publishes all forms related to tanka; therefore we are willing to accept submissions of ryuka. Our guidelines have been updated accordingly.

Also in this issue, we have a tanka sonnet by Jonathan Vos Post on the theme of astronomy. Tanka sonnets can be created in several ways, but the basic form is two tanka plus four lines. The four lines can come at the beginning, middle or end, or can be subdivided into a pair of couplets—whatever serves the subject matter best. Tanka sonnets have occasionally been published; Denis M. Garrison is probably the most notable poet in this regard.

In a continuing development, Autumn Noelle Hall offers 'Conversational Response Tanka,' continuing an approach she began in *Bright Stars 3*. Other poets have done it as well, such as Don Miller's 'On Reading Goldstein's This Short Life' that appeared in *Bright Stars 6*. These ekphrastic tanka partake of the conversational nature of responsive tanka sequences, but the original author is unaware. Thus the conversation is with the poem rather than the poet. This creates a different dynamic within the sequence. Responsive sequences depend upon the relationship between the poets, but ekphrastic tanka responses range widely because the original tanka is a springboard for the responding poet to pursue many lines of thought. (Submissions which include material by more than one author need the permission of all contributors. See the guidelines at AtlasPoetica.org for details.)

Larry Kimmel contributes several cherita, the six line relative of the sedoka, as well as a variation of the sedoka: six lines in three couplets. Sedoka in the original Japanese are composed of two katauta, each of three lines, so sedoka are conventionally divided at the end of line 3. As poets experiment with the sedoka form, it raises the question: what is the defining nature of sedoka? Is it just a free verse written on six short lines? We know that tanka is not a free verse; it is made up of five poetic phrases. Yet the same strictness of form is not seen in the sedoka. Sadly, very few Japanese sedoka are available in translation. Only a handful of sedoka are composed and published in English, therefore it is hard to analyze the form.

Atlas Poetica has always been a home to both innovation and tradition within tanka and related literatures. We have always published original poetry, translations, collaborations, and non-fiction on the subject. We welcome serious attempts to expand our practice and understanding of this ancient literature.

~K~

M. Kei
Editor, Atlas Poetica

Floods cover Bihard India.

Cover Image courtesy of Earth Observatory, NASA.

Alexis Rotella

After every meal
my Italian husband
asks
"Did you have enough
to eat?"

Just a little get together
the neighbors said—
manicured lawn
red velvet cupcakes
served on a silver platter.

Divorce court—
all he asked
was once a week
she launder
his karate gi.

In the moss garden
he tells me
I didn't win
as if to soften
the blow.

The sound of each wave
as it washes ashore—
what is water
but memory
itself.

Bring out
the oil can
the cricket's song
is rusty
tonight.

~United States

Alexis Rotella is a popular poet. Michael McClintock referred to her collection LIP PRINTS as an outstanding example of modern tanka. Rotella practices acupuncture in Arnold, Maryland.

Allistair Wilson

woman up
woman it out
a woman of the world
we'll make a woman of you yet—
grow a pair

marathon runner
weighed down
with charity buckets—
not looking too pleased
to be saving the world

the sparkling fairy dust
of desire
eventually
falls
to the ground

in broken English
the fruit 'n' veg man
struggles to tell a joke
he fluffs . . . I laugh . . . he laughs—
we both pretend

I leave
the kamikaze death-smudge
on my windscreen to remember
fragility . . . suddenness . . . and
the passing of all things

I am
a tanka poet
relax—
I have
been called worse

like trees that get blown
a certain way . . . we too
get blown into a certain shape
and tend—
to stay that way

but . . .
it's not a
proper poem darling
it's only
five lines down!

mouths turn
down
thought
by
thought

while I read your poems
I was a little in love
with you
and even a little
while after

ever since reading
of a man who had his arm
torn off through a car window
I have always been wary
of waving at strangers

the hot summer of '76
parachute training . . . a sprained ankle
forest fires . . . and other fires
burning glances
across awkward discos

five years old
on my tricycle
I cut a worm in half
we had a funeral—
in a matchbox

she banged
dishes together
when she wanted
peace
and quiet

from next door
the reassuring sound
of plates
being slowly
stacked together

on the coast path
a crow stands his ground
for half a second he challenges
for half a second I recognize
my own stroppiness

I dance . . . ooo-eee naked
around the house
to feel winter's first tickle
and freedom
from the norm

in my bamboo garden
of slate and stone
and interesting pieces of wood
a passing cat too
wants to leave his mark

she enters dark crevices
shakes out and burns impurities
then gleefully adds
another skull
to her necklace chain

with my books
and Buddha statues
for years
I've snuffled
around the trough of enlightenment

when the Buddha
fell over in my garden
I didn't go to help him up
I just
accepted it

I gave away
a huge collection of spiritual books
for nothing . . .
free . . .
zilch

the tide is in
the tide is
out
not all days
passed in song

at the end of the day
all words
are dwarfed
by the
setting sun

arms out . . . like zombies
the electorate head towards
the polling station
burgers . . . . coke . . . burgers . . . coke
burgers . . . coke . . .

being a vegetarian
didn't stop her
from boiling
her vegetables
to death

you thought I could
be a man
of greatness—
I agreed . . . .
I'm absolutely full of . . . *ness*

ah . . . for the piece of clothing
that acts
like a girdle
without actually
looking like one

haiku poet
chokes
to death
on
cherry blossoms

as advised . . . I danced . . .
'as if no one is looking'
and cleared
a nice circle
around me

not a fanatic
I weigh myself once a month
making sure
to take off even
the lightest socks

it's true
I'm different
but that's only because
I've been through the desert
on a fish with no name

using apple cider vinegar
I removed five hundred warts
from under my armpits . . . .
not really—I just wanted
to see the look on your face

sorry
but I
can't see
what the
delusion is

I am a peaceful man
but if I keep hearing
'the attitude governs the altitude'
I am going to have
to put a gun against your head

I'm not saying
I am set in my ways
but I am thinking
of naming the house
'Sabre Tooth'

the pubs
are rough
around here—
5pm to 7pm it's
snappy hour

I wanted
to know love . . . .
you wanted to know—
how long
was left on my mortgage

testosterone
and a pretty face
lord I tried
lord
I tried

even at a ripe-ish age
I still practice my
little-boy-lost-look—
you never know when
you may need some . . . female sympathy!

~United Kingdom

*Allistair Wilson has previously published in Bright Stars 7 and issues
20 and 21 of Atlas Poetica; A Journal of World Tanka. He lives In
Kent South East England.*

Andrew Howe

lounge room drinks
drown the evening news
so adult
your conversation
an approaching storm

lunchbreak
wet foot shoppers scurry
. . . unseen
a blind woman
sidesteps pavement puddles

unanswered
the bullfrog's croak echoes—
alone
in the crowd
my lily pond life

~Australia

From now on

Andrew Howe & *Vyonne McLelland-Howe*

slipper polished
knotted floorboards
creak . . .
harshly daybreak
lengthens her routine

shards of light
slice the darkness
piercing
my illusion of sleep
awakening to a world of pain

tattooed dots
on her chest
pinpoint
a firing range—
her reddened skin will never tan

from now on
shunning the midday sun
we learn
. . . to love again
the paler version of me

~Australia

Vyonne McLelland-Howe lives in Wollongong in New South Wales, on the eastern coast of Australia. She is retired and finds great pleasure in writing tanka. Her tanka have been published in Australian and international publications.

Andrew Howe is an Australian naval officer who lives in NSW. His interests include military history, geology, and reading and writing tanka.

Andy McCall

gentle
little bird
dead
his earthly body still
only his spirit flies

he wants
to be with her
he struggles
to show his love
in his dark times

alone in the house
I look to the garden
glad of the soft light
of the burning candle—
she is at peace in the holy

in the quiet of evening
reflecting on his life
the man
finds comfort
with the woman he loves

the evening is still
darkness gathers in
before bed
one last feed for the birds
this is the holy place

~Norwich, England

Andy McCall lives with his wife Joy in Norwich, England. He works for the local council. In his spare time he rides motocross and he loves to spend time in the countryside. He loves all creatures, especially his scruffy cat. He likes to cook, and he bakes bread. He has occasionally written longer poems, but lately he began to write tanka as a way of expressing his tangled feelings. He likes country music, old movies, and home.

smörgåsbord

Autumn Noelle Hall

I watch episode after episode of Henning Mankell's *Wallander*, tailing Detective Kurt and his faithful dog, Jussi, along the Ysad coastline until I am rocking with the gentle wave-song that is Swedish. It matters not that this is a cop drama —albeit that beautiful rough-cut continental kind, where actors are allowed to stubble their beards and paunch their guts—or that every rusty coil of humanity's twisted heart is pulled taut, heat-straightened and made to gleam, murder by gruesome murder. I somehow fall in love a little with these provincial streets, those weathered faces, that dark humor. Even so, it is the language that sweeps me away, blooms its golden rapeseed acres across the grey horizon of my linguist brain; awakens this desire to eavesdrop on water cooler banter, to order a dozen sugared *klejner* to pass around the station, to share a late night round after the bust—*skål*!

after *tack* for thanks
after *hej* for hello
is it *ingenting*
I recognize at first
—nothing

~*Pikes Peak Region, Colorado, USA*

I've been through the desert on a horse with no name . . .*

Autumn Noelle Hall

After several years journeying, during which time I've made countless suggestions, answered endless questions, sent multiple links to dozens of resources, provided copious explanations and hands-on how-to's for each and every poem he's sent—and even suggested he join the Society (comping him copies of the journals), he asks if the jo is merely an excuse to add a non-sequitur.

So I've decided to put him down.

a nightmare
trying to explain
dreaming room . . .
tired of leading this horse
to water he just won't drink

*from the 1972 Gold Single A Horse with No Name by the band
America*

~*Pikes Peak Region, Colorado, USA*

Autumn Noelle Hall lives in Green Mountain Falls, Colorado, with her husband, daughters, and their rapscallion Australian Shepherd. When not feeding the birds or photographing the mountains, she writes. A Pikes Peak Arts Council nominee for Page Poet of the Year, Autumn is honored to have had her work included in many fine Asian Short Form publications both at home and abroad. She is especially grateful to you, the readers, who bring her words to life.

Autumn Noelle Hall

flicker
clinging to the drain pipe
hammering away
the way my ex thought
loud and hard were sexy

I waste
precious energy ranting
on about shoes
until his tanka
puts a sock in it

in league with Frieda
I refuse to wax
my mustache
the way we women
suffer for our art

magnesium glass
purpling in the sun
some bruises
take decades
to come to light

piercing her body
over and over she tries
to impale
the memory of her first
forced piercing

hoping
her anti-possession tattoo
liberates her
from her own
darkness

the father's gun
found with his son
at the skatepark
his board, darkside
in the half-pipe

—for Caleb

ink dark
these half moons beneath my eyes . . .
insomnia
the doctor remarks
but I know it's just tanka

~Green Mountain Falls, Colorado, USA

Conversational Response Tanka

Autumn Noelle Hall

I toast
my continental consort
who assures me
the perfect breast
would just fill a champagne glass

—in response to Don Miller's I was going to read, Bright Stars 7

mocking my mowing
dad describes its abstract art
the roundabout swaths
I cut through our yard
avoiding the daylilies

—in response to Don Miller's no reason needed, Bright Stars 7

the marked drop
since she left for college
in blood pressure
and grocery costs
and ab-toning laughter

—in response to Don Miller's how many points, Simply Haiku, Vol 7 no 1

~Green Mountain Falls, Colorado, USA

Housework

Autumn Noelle Hall

I am Switzerland
asleep on my office floor
while you lie
in our bed next door
at war with yourself

salt talks
the tub jets' white noise
drowning the silence
you focusing on you
enough for both of us

heavy-duty
that load you are loathe
to admit
all this round-and-round
before coming clean

you see the rust
in the brillo pad's dish
but miss the gleam
of the stainless steel pots
drip-drying on the drainboard

all that glitters
the glass sparkling, winking
like those diamonds
I never asked for
in this second life

I could no more
crochet cardigans
from dryer lint
than reknit us both
into our unworn selves

how foolish of me
to believe I knew you
just because
I knew myself . . . our names
criss-crossed in the dust

your little checkmarks
pinning down passages
in a thousand books
could it be so straightforward
learning to read you better . . . ?

turning my plants
away from the window
to help them grow
would facing your dark side
do the same for you . . . ?

no end to housework
again these plates these mugs
this silverware
feeding the emptiness
only eats us alive

~Green Mountain Falls, Colorado, USA

A Body in Fukushima

Autumn Noelle Hall & Don Miller

An ekphrastic tanka collaboration in response to the joint exhibition of the same title by photographer William Johnston and dancer Eiko Otake

sōteigai
beyond conception they said
of Daiichi's doom
Johnston's lens bringing
Fukushima into focus

through his looking glass
these nightmarish images
if only
upon waking
they ceased to exist

no shutter
long enough to capture
these ghosts
possessing Eiko's body
persuading her to dance

writhing
on a platform
bathed
with unseen chemicals
she spills onto the rails

living vines
belie the ashen anguish
binding her
to the rusting ways
of train-less tracks

with gnarled hand
she reaches
for the vanishing point
a half-life
millions of years away

fingers that swirled
a million grains of rice
through clouding water
grasp now for clarity
in a poisoned puddle-mirror

withered
she stands with sunflowers
in Fukushima
drawing a poison
from the land

how many seeds
rooting here: in a phone booth
there: in a child's toy
the radiation blooms
watered by her tears

this wave of horror
breaking
on her face
before
the surging tide

now, a fallen bird
washed up on the sand . . .
her wing-like arm waves
against the devil wind
mad-dancing in her hair

caped arms
spread crane-like
her mourning stance
held
for eternity

cradling
a red scarf bundle
to her cheek . . .
no holding back this tide
of impending unborn

little hope
for the twins
born too soon
but still
the candles burn . . .

~Fukushima, Japan (as witnessed from Colorado and
New Mexico, USA)

Note: Autumn and Don would like to encourage readers to
seek out the images which inspired this work in the galleries
and films available at: http://eikoandkoma.org/
abodyinfukushima

Autumn Noelle Hall lives in a cabin in Green Mountain Falls,
Colorado, with her husband, daughters, and their Aussie, Indigo. When
not feeding birds or photographing the mountains, she writes. A Pikes
Peak Arts Council nominee for Page Poet of the Year, Autumn is
honored to have her work included in many fine Asian Short Form
publications, both at home and abroad. She is especially grateful to you,
Readers, for bringing her words to life.

Don Miller lives in southern New Mexico, USA. He has been writing
tanka since the early 1980s when he learned about the poetic form
while attending Purdue University. Don has had his tanka, tanka prose,
haiku, haibun and other poems published in various print and online
journals over the past decade or so.

Other People's Trash

Bill Waters

When you're a boy, trash is treasure. I remember walking to school one day with my best friend—when was it? third grade, maybe?—and we saw a smashed plastic ship model lying on the curb beside some empty trash cans. There were planks and spars and tangles of rigging and, to our great delight, a double-handful of tiny cannons.

We gathered up what we could and hurried on to school with our booty. Over the next couple days, we combed the grass for any further bits of ship debris as we passed by until a lawnmower told us more decisively than words that we would find no more pieces.

I still have one of those cannons—the sole surviving relic of a distant memory and a valued piece of flotsam from the lost world of boyhood.

> sea spray
> and the sting
> of blowing sand . . .
> even a broken clock
> can't stop the tick of time

~Burlington County, New Jersey, USA

Writing the Final Chapter?

Bill Waters

No one's wishing for a nuclear winter, but we're not hoping for the incremental extinction of global warming, either—a summer of sorts, and a death by degrees.

Too much pollution, too much fixation on consumerism and quarterly profits . . . Is this how human history will end? In a drawn-out, slow-motion moment of self-destruction? Or will we, against all odds, unite for the common good and save our planet—and ourselves?

> silence now
> where once the brook . . .
> coyotes
> have been sighted
> near the interstate

~Mercer County, New Jersey, USA

Bill Waters, a lifelong poet and writer, lives in Pennington, New Jersey, USA, with his wonderful wife and their three amazing cats.

Bruce England

Every day
I eat
I win over
being eaten
until I don't

A small troop
of hominids stopped
in a shallow stream
they drank and left
their footprints for us

The raccoon hand
tied to the raccoon brain
when we are gone
they could evolve into
something like us

In the presence
of eternity
the mountains
are as transient
as the clouds

So much
depends
upon
a mailbox
in the rain

The trees,
shrubs, flowers
all seem
to lean toward me
to comfort me

Precious—
a few lines
of my life
in a journal
of tanka

From darkness
I squirmed through
my mother's wormhole
into this dream ball
of earth-water-wind-fire

Getting gas
I didn't intend this
but now
I'm taking
the long way home

Go ahead
put flowers
in my coffin
my sinuses
won't care

Coming
in behind
reciting poetry
from a book
on her back

Sedoka

Bruce England

One hundred million
years ago, a storm washed
a horseshoe crab into
a toxic lagoon
it lived long enough to leave
a thirty-two foot death crawl

~*United States*

*Bruce England lives and works in Silicon Valley. His haiku writing
began in 1984, and his serious tanka writing in 2010. Other related
interests include haiku theory and practice. Long ago, a chapbook,
Shorelines, was published with a friend, Tony Mariano.*

Carole Johnston

crayons
like Eliot's cats
need names
not only Crayola names
I write their secret colors

I want all
those green and gold boxes
on the shelf
inhale the scent of rainbow
my fingers touch each color

I pull
out crayons one by one
sniff them
roll each around my hands
choose cerulean—turquoise

'purple eyes'
morning glory violet ink
glass jar on my desk
fingers clutch crayons
and fountain pen

I want to
smear daffodil crayon
all over
this rainy grey day
paint butterfly balloons

clutching my
'sonic silver' crayon
I float clouds
the color of thunder
explode white lightning

which one
is the Haiku crayon
living
in color of the moment
'thunder blue' or 'witchy green'

a crayon called
'the moon bleeds silver'
keeps me awake
trying to write the face
of a new born child

in my book
I color green synapses
sparking words
inside the brains of poets
a crayon called 'mystery'

'rumbling sludge'
crayon smudges the mountain's
'coal black eye'
colors for strip mining
Appalachia's pearly tears

'spring burst'
'dogwood salmon'
street sketch
my 'cherry blossom crayon'
fading shades of April

'African mask red'
juxtaposed with ivy green
on my back porch
cardinals nesting in the vines
a crayon's deep heart

'dead chipmunk'
soulful striped crayon
rusty earth
and burnt sienna
dark side of the sun

drawing with
your 'tarot card' crayon
call it 'vision'
clear as candle wax
stay away from the flame

some crayons called
'sweet cacophony'
'birdsong bluejay'
'cardinal' 'wren' and best
the 'crow at sunrise'

stone white crayons
'jesus dogwood green'
'holy river'
I drive through a memory
of gratitude and rain

in space between
sky blue and cerulean
silence
a crayon called 'nowhere zen'
another one called 'bliss'

if I were a crayon
I would fly up like butterflies
right out of the box
melting in sunflowers
call me 'mariposa'

the shock
of a thousand daffodils
my 'inner Wordsworth'
crayon wanders 'cloud lonely'
into everybody's inner child

a crayon called
'flame' lights up my mornings
'butter yellow'
sun streams through sparrowsong
the world spins and glows

Walt Whitman's
favorite electric crayons
'violet grass'
'Lincoln lilacs blooming'
and still more pain in April

in a sketch book
crayons called 'riots & death'
broad waxy strokes
of 'smoke' and 'charred ruins'
too much crimson and black

Jersey Shore sunrise
all crayons in the box
can't capture it
my memories 'gull blue'
and 'tangerine joy'

Baltimore burning
I use the same colors
as ocean sunrise
crayons named 'pleasure'
'pain' same hues different tone

Buzzfeed wants
to tell me the color
of my 'soul' but
my 'essence-blueluminous'
glowing in the crayon box

bruise on the city
a crayon called 'police blue'
crushes the scene
'midnight riot' draws chaos
across neon billboards

naming crayons
'stained glass' 'dream mandala'
melted wax
flowing down a bottle
I call it 'Matisse in May'

~United States

Carole Johnston enjoys driving, being lost, writing haiku and tanka. Her chapbook, Journeys: Getting Lost, was recently published by Finishing Line Press and is available from Amazon. She is a retired creative writing teacher, living in Lexington, Kentucky, but her home is "nowhere zen New Jersey."

Chen-ou Liu

stitch after stitch
in the clothes I wear,
hope against hope
I will soon return home . . .
Mother alone on the shore

after the divorce
I run into my first love
on a misty night
like kids we play
Chinese Whisper

~*Taipei, Taiwan*

walking home
from the last night shift . . .
I hold a copy
of my first chapbook
like the harvest of sorrow

long break
after my ESL* class . . .
nostalgia
walks in like a leper
with a warning bell

ESL stands for English as a Second Language.

I say firmly,
I can start over again . . .
their doubt
creeps in with each bite
of a bitter melon

Golden Arches
against the winter sky . . .
in the break room
a co-worker and I
share one Happy Meal

beneath the lamppost—
the cardboard sign
on her chest
reads *Wearth/Worth**
in black and gold

The Old English word wearth means outcast.

~*Toronto, Ontario, Canada*

loneliness
selects its own society
in the attic . . .
cold moon in the window,
water-stained ceiling and me

I look tenderly
at this woman
who can't look back:
the framed photo
of my youthful ex

returned manuscript
on the coffee-stained desk . . .
her words, *I see
the phoenix in you,*
linger on this cold night

old boxed set
of *Marcel Proust*
on the bed
my memory of Taipei
framed by an attic window

~*Ajax, Ontario, Canada*

waking
next to a stranger
with no clothes on . . .
the afternoon sun
deepens the silence

~*Wasaga Beach, Ontario, Canada*

Sociolinguistics 101: No Language Is Neutral

Chen-ou Liu

for Dionne Brand

ESL class at dusk:
white flight
from my Chinese mouth
to her Canadian ears
white fright

his parting words
like wet snow
blanket my world:
It's a cappuccino, Liu
not a cup of chino

"I used to be"
are dirty words to her ears—
I leave my baggage
at the door of no return
and clean my eyes

do, does, did, done
screaming in my head . . .
can one ideogram
   this   做 (zuo)
muffle their voices?

Oh, you write
in English . . .
his "oh"
tasting like pinot noir
left open overnight

You're a poet?
I dabble in the dark arts . . .
in her eyes
I'm a Chinese coolie
working in the English mine

the Chinese
erased from the "last spike" photo . . . *
out of revenge
I write a "white fl/right" verse
stamped Made in Canada

* The "last spike" refers to the ceremonial final spike driven into the Canadian Pacific Railway at 9:22 am on November 7, 1885.

~Toronto; Ajax, Ontario, Canada

Chen-ou Liu lives in Ajax, Ontario, Canada. He is the author of five books, including Following the Moon to the Maple Land (First Prize, 2011 Haiku Pix Chapbook Contest) and A Life in Transition and Translation (Honorable Mention, 2014 Turtle Light Press Biennial Haiku Chapbook Competition), His tanka and haiku have been honored with many awards.

Dave Read

after our first
ride of the season
treads of
my cycling shorts
mark my spare tire

flipping ahead
through my empty journal
the thoughts
I have not,
not had yet

leafing through
a coupon book
she complains
of the ways I
still sell her short

preaching
against religion
the young man
wearing
a Jesus beard

sprouting like
weeds at the gate
landscapers
wanting to
clean up my lawn

over a late night
plate of nachos
I listen
to an infomercial
describe my fitness dreams

seeing her
grey hair turn
silver
the moonlight slips
through the blinds

opening up
a metal chair
she invites
me to sit through
one hard-assed discussion

passing another
patch of roadside lilies
from the comfort
of my car these
poems about nature

a week old mango
rots in the bowl
I do not
believe what he
says about passion

stretched as
wide as the horizon
the promise
I never
kept with myself

the moon fades
into the day sky
her initial
enthusiasm
nowhere to be seen

against the long
pull of the rake
the short
pull of muscles
seizing in my back

waking at
the crack of dawn
to the sounds
of the chicken I
undercooked last night

the sun
drops past a rim
of clouds
they shoot hoops
by streetlight

no longer
native to the area
mountains
known by
their European names

completing its
journey back to earth
this bag
of garden soil
purchased at Costco

~Canada

*Dave Read is a Canadian poet whose work has appeared in many
journals, including Atlas Poetica. You can view his tanka and
micropoetry on Twitter, @AsSlimAsImBeing.*

Three days of Rain

David Klasovsky

turning on my heels;
what was that I passed
hurrying to the city?
a cloud of white moths dancing
through yellow mustard flowers

high fences winding
around green fields and playgrounds
the sweet smell of grass
and children's voices follow
the stranger on the highway

sparrows and pigeons
gather around the benches
old friends milk laughter
from gossip and memories;
day grows cold, the sky golden

in a bed of leaves
blown against the building
a steady buzz protests
the gardener's rake, the wind:
here wild bees are nesting

beyond: lie slate skies;
above, among clustered leaves
round as grubs and pink
the first mulberries glisten.
the path is sodden, littered

the old gardener's
stood a single stone erect
amid his flowers—
he's elevated his art!
or: marks his summer's passing—

down the tumulus
across the tracks, through briars
sits a stone that juts
into the water; to sit
above the dizzy current!

across the river
in another, darker cave
another hermit
scribbles on his pad and dreams
of dark wine sipped and toasts raised

up the hill come three
children with bright colored hoops
they bump each other
now one leads now another
and then—they pass out of view—

white petals: litter
the sidewalk; the first victim
of summer's first rain
is spring's first precocious rose—
a sun-kissed breeze will scatter these

a heavy-headed
camellia kisses earth.
a garden well kept
still keeps its secrets. sun, rain
nourish here; and wreak havoc—!

a dark thread of cloud
divides the moon in two.
the distant city
is silent; from the near woods
soft laughter, gentle voices

a soft beam of sun
aslant finds its way to me
through the green forest;
through the sullen skies; past worlds
unknown—to this dark place

the twisted blankets
of my bed lie in sunlight.
in shadow i write
in a half-full old notebook;
recording my dreams—I pause—

leaning from the bridge
to watch the swirling current—
on the ivied bank
a floral patterned mattress;
across the river—a train . . .

an earthen path winds
behind red brick apartments
mid-morning quiet;
a single old man, straw hat,
formal clothes, stops, bows his head

sleeping stone lions
guard a red graveled garden
petals of flowers—
white pink lavender yellow—
lie there like dreams remembered

back and forth through town
getting little done, on some streets
roses arc over
the sidewalk; i play a game—
matching colors to fragrance

birds and travelers
at the bus stop; teenagers press
into the sweetshop
the sidewalk rack gets hustled
back into the seamstress's shop

it won't stop raining
grey skies, grey streets; a black car
stops motor running;
an olive skinned girl in pink
and purple comes hurrying

experience leads
a man to stick to safe roads;
here's me, short of breath,
giddy, tempted, listening
for the splash of new rainfall

tires sizzle through
fresh puddles; neon lights
wake within twilight—
along the edge of night paths
parallel—might briefly merge—

the morning wind skirts
the glade, finds the treetops, spins
new leaves—just enough
to show their silvery sides;
leafed limbs sway like tethered clouds—

~United States

David Klasovsky has created innovative, often anonymous work in new mediums and old; he is generally wary of the public eye. Born in Ohio, he has traveled extensively in the Middle East, and now works as a writer and dramaturge in New York. He is at present writing an account of political encoding in theater, comparing that of America in the HUAC years with that of the Early Modern period.

Foundering

Debbie Strange

this is how
to make your deathbed
this is the way
you fold transgressions
into hospital corners

this is how
to write your death poem
this is the way
you hold your last breath
when the plug is pulled

~*Winnipeg, Manitoba, Canada*

Debbie Strange lives in Winnipeg, Manitoba, Canada. She is a member of the Writers' Collective of Manitoba and the Manitoba Writers' Guild, and is affiliated with several haiku and tanka organizations. Her writing has received awards, and has appeared in numerous journals. Debbie is an avid photographer whose images have been published and exhibited. You are invited to view her haiga on Twitter @Debbie_Strange. Keibooks is releasing Debbie's first collection of tanka this summer.

Elizabeth Howard

screech-owl moon—
bony legs protruding
from the mud-daubed chimney,
I crouch in the corner
of the dilapidated house

vacant cabin—
in the dim light
a maze of spider silk,
giant spiders sparring
over tiny bones

sleepless night—
somewhere a distant yodel
a song of grief unbounded . . .
later a phantom at the window
wailing of treachery

town square . . .
every Saturday
the old country preacher
counted the wages of sin
his hoarse voice blowing in the wind

back from the war
she can tell no one
of the sexual assault,
but when she closes her eyes
a giant hand grips her throat

caught between the horses
and the wild geese
I stand transfixed
a pillar of fear
until the dust settles

after the accident
snowy bouquets mushroom
the raw red earth—
yet snow can cover
neither grief nor guilt

in a desolate castle
she struggles up
the same spiral staircase
continuously
never reaching the top

as filmy curtains part
a razor in a bony hand
slashes my red curls . . .
I flee the rickety house
strewing coils of fire

a moonbow lighting
the waterfall spray . . .
once a fabled mermaid
washed her long hair
by this misty boulder

still attached
to the umbilicus cord
the fetus found in the trash . . .
girls huddle about my desk
questioning . . .

spare room
crates of dreams
dust motes of words
all the promises
never fulfilled

~*United States*

Collateral Damage

Elizabeth Howard

shot saving his students . . .
so many blooms on his grave
one for every child
to whom he revealed
the secrets of mathematics

atop the book shelves
an alabaster girl
reading for pleasure—
yet how have we come to this?
a girl may die for a book?

air strike . . .
the target still standing
but, oh!
the collateral damage
a schoolyard of children

~United States

Elizabeth Howard lives in Crossville, Tennessee. Her tanka have been published in Eucalypt, red lights, Mariposa, Ribbons, Gusts, Atlas Poetica, Skylark, Moonbathing, and other journals.

Grunge

didn't know
rabbits could growl
till i denied
a tiny lop
a cookie

excited for my brother's
part on prime time tv
till i hear that
his skin has cast him as
khalid the bombmaker

can't work till
i can see a doctor;
can't see a doctor
till i can work
to pay for it

forced to ask
the same people we're
protesting against
whether we can legally
stage the protest

protests against
poverty and inequality
shut down by
charging the protestors
a fine to rejoin it

we were violent
juvenile delinquents
fleeing from our
first encounter with
a harmless glow worm

my hell is not an inferno
but the knowledge of
what I could have achieved
had i been able to
live up to my potential

~United States

Grunge is a gay Indo-American tanka poet, with an interest in bugs, body modifications, and the end of the world.

Two Hundred Millimetres

Gerry Jacobson

summer comes in
all too soon this year
Gaia broods
in sultry stillness
ants scurry busily

waking slowly
to the raven's caw
opening my eyes
to a grey morning
and gentle drizzle

cold kiss
of rain on my face
along the ridge
rainwashed thoughts
'neath a Gore-Tex hood

six days
without the sun
my heart sings
this blessed La Niña—
two hundred millimetres

after the drought
walking across wet grass
through Yellow Box
and Blakely's Gum
magpies and butcher birds

~Canberra, ACT, Australia

Shiva Nataraja

Gerry Jacobson

Often stopped to admire it. Wrote tanka about it. Well, it's a favourite image. And *Shiva Nataraja* is one of my favourite yoga poses. And don't I often feel that I'm Lord of the Dance?

moving
from deep within
becoming
the dancer
lost in its ecstasy

What a shock when newspaper reports appear. The much loved statue is believed looted from a temple in an Indian village. Our National Gallery paid $5m for it. The American dealer is on trial for theft. Gallery highly embarrassed. Director might resign. The statue is removed from display. Returned to India.

four bronze arms
hold up the cosmos
Shiva
lord of the dance
Creator . . . Destroyer

~Canberra, Australia

Side Effects

Gerry Jacobson

Surgery stings. Even elective surgery like a hernia repair. I could have got away without it, for years perhaps. But the hernia inhibited my movement, in the dance, and bushwalking. Now it's done and I'm coming back to life. Resurgent. Three or four grey days sleeping it off. Tail end of the cyclonic rain up north. Anaesthesia and trauma dissolving down here. Interesting side effects. Well, the surgeon did warn me.

> I am a man
> of swollen testes
> my scrotum hangs
> all black and blue . . .
> try and dull the pain with panadeine

~Canberra, ACT, Australia

Gerry Jacobson writes tanka in the cafes of three cities. Canberra, where he lives. Sydney and Stockholm, where his grandchildren live. He just published a chapbook 'Dancing with Another Me', a collection of 'tanka prose' about dance.

Janet Butler

even this
has its story
your scarf
of intricate design
left unfinished

he's taut
like an engine growling
at a long red light
ready to burn rubber
at the wrong word

trees
push up against
the café window
students buried in books
oblivious to spring

he floats
on the surface
of their life
the deep hook of old sins
keeping him tethered

fog rolls in
and squats, a fat buddha,
indifferent as he
pulls color and shadow
into a gray nirvana

~Alameda, California, USA

Janet Butler began writing tanka in September of 2014, and feels the tanka form congenial to her love of short, intense poetry, dense with meaning.

Janet Lynn Davis

the still life
I painted at sixteen
. . . all this time
hanging in my parents' house,
soaking up their hues

~family home, Houston, Texas, USA

more timid
about the cold water
in this lagoon
than mingling with stingrays,
velvet against my skin

~island in the Bahamas

golden-winged
a small bird skims
the ocean,
dipping into the blue
for bits of sustenance

~Southern Caribbean Sea

setting up
for a Sunday jazz brunch
in the park—
overhead, the notes
of wild parakeets

~Fort Lauderdale, Florida, USA

a dollop
of clotted cream
on my scone—
the pleasant taste of things
I once avoided

~afternoon tea, cruise ship

grouped by class
while on the *Titanic*
though just one
set of numbers
for all their gravestones

~Titanic cemetery, Halifax, Nova Scotia, Canada

cloudless sky—
I capture my shadow
in a photo,
placing hand on hip
to show some attitude

~home, Grimes County, Texas, USA

the tree man
identifies our sapling . . .
walnut
an exotic word
amid these oaks and pines

~home, Grimes County, Texas, USA

Janet Lynn Davis lives with her husband in a quiet rustic community north of Houston, Texas. Since childhood, she's had a strong interest in the written word as both art form and means of communication. Her poetry has appeared in numerous journals, anthologies, and other venues. She currently serves as the vice president of the Tanka Society of America.

Meta-Sonnet: "Pluto and Eris"

Jonathan Vos Post

Pluto and Eris
are the largest Trans-Neptunian objects
though several others come close—
Makemake, Naumea & Namaka,
Salacia, Sedna, Orcus, Vanth, Quaoar & Weywot

Methane ice
on Pluto, the only other: Titan,
of solid bodies
of the Outer Solar System—
welcome to the Kuiper Belt

July 2015
NASA's New Horizons
spacecraft shall complete
first reconnaissance of a Kuiper Belt Planet

Jonathan Vos Post is: co-author with Ray Bradbury; co-author with Richard Feynman, Nobel Laureate physicist; co-editor with David Brin and Arthur C. Clarke; co-broadcaster with Isaac Asimov quoted by name in Robert Heinlein's "Expanded Universe"; Winner of 1987 Rhysling Award for Best Science Fiction Poem of Year; Published in Nebula Awards Anthology #23, 1989; Semifinalist for 1996 Nebula Award; Part-time Professor (at 5 colleges and universities) His Tanka have appeared in venues such as: Tanka in M. Kei, Editor, All the Shells : The Tanka Society of America's Member Anthology for 2014

the bard

Joy McCall

I was almost twelve, tired of a diet of what schools think kids should learn, and exploring the kind of poetry that sang to my heart.

I handed in this tanka for homework. I got the cane for being disrespectful to the sacred Bard.

It was a long time before I learned that tanka shouldn't rhyme.

William Shakespeare
I do not like you
Shelley, please get lost
read me Tu Fu and Li Po
teach me Rumi and Frost

~Norwich, England

pair

Joy McCall

he says *no*
I say then when I die
my bones will rattle
every night at his door
until daybreak

and my blood
will flow under the sill
and cover the floor
and I will breathe the cold air
of the grave on his fair face

~Norwich, England

VOWS

Joy McCall

from the broken shed
the woodland path
leads uphill
to an old chapel,
a plain meeting house

the man and woman
are making vows
at the altar
the purple-robed priest
is large and a little drunk

the pews
are thick with dust
and covered
with the small footprints
of rats and birds

three sheep
are huddled together
by the font
there is a smell
of damp wool and incense

promises
have been offered
to the gods
the priest bows his head
and says the prayers

the couple
are leaving, and still
he prays
it is what priests do
he knows little else

the chapel door
stands open for decades
birds and bats
fly in and out; the sheep lie,
bones under the font

~Norfolk, England

painters

Joy McCall

The father and daughter, painters and
decorators, had been working all day, painting
my sanctuary in a soft cream colour.
When they said goodbye and arranged to
return the next day, I went to the room to see
what they had done.
It didn't seem like much, for what they were
charging me for the job.
I looked around, disappointed, and then I
saw a book on a dust-sheet on a chair . . .

painters
not achieving much
then I find
'January'
with cream fingerprints

thanks a lot, M. Kei

~Norwich, England

the words of the preacher . . .

Joy McCall

found tanka, Ecclesiastes 3, the King James Bible

to every thing
there is a season
and a time
to every purpose
under the heaven:

a time to be born
a time to die
a time to plant
a time to pluck up
that which is planted

a time to kill
a time to heal
a time
to break down
a time to build up

a time to weep
a time to laugh
a time
to mourn
a time to dance

a time to cast away stones
a time to gather stones together
a time to embrace
a time to refrain
from embracing

a time to get
a time to lose
a time to keep
and a time
to cast away

a time to rend
a time to sew
a time
to keep silence
a time to speak

a time to love
a time to hate
a time of war
and a time of peace . . .
and everything beautiful in its time

~Norwich, England

shell and book

Joy McCall

there are
tales to be told
in the poet's gifts:
the words have not come
well to me, yet . . .

for Liam

my thumbpad
rests in the dip
in the hollow
where it finds
its home

it is half
of a bivalve
long-smoothed
by the salt sea
and the poet's hands

my thumb settled,
a long fingernail
explores
the other side,
convex, ridged

there is
a thin tapping into
the deeper grooves
nail talking to shell
five furrows, like a poem

shell in one hand
book in the other
I read :
I grow old among
the mist, the river, the stones *

from the far east
the winds bring the voice
of a long-dead nun:
the noise of drums and oars
make it difficult to sleep *

* *'Daughters of Emptiness' by Beata Grant*

~*Norwich, England*

all fall down

Joy McCall

I said *in the midst*
of life we are in death
and he smiled
and said *in the midst*
of death we are in life

sometimes
in mid-winter
summer shows up—
those sudden bright days
that melt the snow

and in summer
winter can close in
with bitter cold
and the discontent
of which the bard spoke

sometimes
in a strangely dry April
leaves fall
and half the shrub
is brown and dead

and I have seen
in late October
new shoots
on the lavender
and on the wild thyme

on a joyful day
I have felt a stab of pain
a funeral hymn
mingling with the
sea chantey I'm humming

and while
a dark dirge is playing
in my head
out of the blue comes a line
of a nursery rhyme

inside me
a small child, laughing
ring around the rosy
and the woman, knowing
we must *all fall down*

~Norwich, England

violets and bones

Joy McCall

it is midnight
the light is out
the room is dark
I am making poems
about trees and mystery

everywhere
there are people
doing things—
working and sleeping
and fighting and dying

there is a boat
loaded with migrants
it is sinking
they will all die
even the children

and yet
I go on lying here
writing poems
what do my words matter
with all that death?

there are the bones
of the dead everywhere
there will be mine
before too long—
will the poems matter then?

I read Han Shan,
poems from Cold Mountain
and I think
of all the million bones
picked clean since then

so it is midnight
and I write poems
what else can I do?
I cannot rescue
the dark drowning children

there are
wild violets
in the garden
they cast off seeds
and spread over the stones

every year
there will be more violets
and more bones
and more poems
and many more dark midnights

~Norwich, England

madness

Joy McCall

the place feels
a little crazy
these days
reality is
slipping downstream

the sorrows
have pulled at the water
as the moon does
the flow speeds up
rushing to the sea

there is madness
in the old city
voices and faces
the bickering
of mating birds and men

there is no
full risen moon
to excuse us
no hunger or thirst
no loss of life or limb

it is spring
and there is madness
everywhere
I sit in the garden
counting violets

~Norwich, England

apocalypse

Joy McCall

it is no good
he tells me, to hide
in the house
under the bed
or in the cupboard

the zombies
can hear my heartbeat
through the walls
there is no escaping
their infected bites

they swarm
over the land
contagious
heartless, their mad eyes
searching for prey

the only hope
when they come
snarling
is to kill, with crossbows
and heavy swords

even then, the evil
spreads and festers
hope dies
man and zombies all succumb . . .
the land is black with death

~Norwich, England

Inspired by Jake Street.

enso

Joy McCall

the snake
turning back
upon himself
writhing, coiling
biting his own tail

he leaves
the husk drying
in the sun
slips into the long grass
to die of his own venom

she watches, stretches
and slides her soft length
inside his shed skin
she fits her gold eyes
into empty sockets

dying scales cling
drawing blood, sucking life . . .
the new snake slithers,
hungry, out from the darkness
into the new day

~Norwich, England

Common Lane

Joy McCall

for centuries
this patch of land
this wild plot
between cemetery
and river, has not changed

in the midst
of this settlement,
this thorpe, *
the long sloping meadow,
woods and thickets

the winding track
trodden by common people
and livestock
a good grazing land
a slow bathing place

it is sold now
to cold developers
for the building
of river-front homes
for the pampered rich

bulldozers rumble
a great swathe is cleared
a barren slope
the dear narrow dirt-lane
now wide enough for limousines

we complain
bitterly, the council
pays no heed
money talks
bricks and mortar win

we watch as trees fall
nests, chicks, eggs scattered
in the mud
badgers' setts destroyed
fox cubs dead in the dens

my heart aches
and in sleepless nights
all I hear
is the cruel slow-dying of life
and Common sense

*thorpe is a variant of the Middle English word thorp,
meaning hamlet or small village*

~Thorpe St. Andrew, Norwich, England

following the deer

Joy McCall

night pain
too sharp for peace
I left my bed
and fled to where
the deer were running

up the long slope
into the fir trees
where the wind lives
along the hard path
trodden by many hooves

and I heard
an old voice speaking:
he makes my feet
like the feet of the deer
and sets me on a high place

and the voice sang:
gentleness
has made me great
and we fly
on the wings of the wind

and in the deep wood
the old one said: *darkness*
is his secret place,
about him are dark waters
and thick clouds of the skies

and there were
hailstones and coals of fire
splitting the darkness . . .
and sweet under my feet
the stony path of the deer

Italics from Psalm 18, the King James Bible.

~*Norwich, England*

on the 13th anniversary of the crash

Joy McCall

this morning
the pale sun melts
that thin shell
it breaks the surface
of loss and pain

my fingers
reach in and touch
the old ashes of grief . . .
even in that cold dark place
they burn and burn

I want to walk

~*Norwich, England*

Joy McCall is a nurse/counsellor, retired because of paraplegia following a motorcycle crash. She has written all kinds of poetry for 50 years, publishing occasionally here and there. She lives on the edge of the old walled city of Norwich, England, having spent much of her life in Canada. She treasures most her loved ones, nature, books, words and tattoos, life, and poetry. Keibooks published her 'circling smoke, scattered bones', 'hedgerows' and 'rising mist, fieldstones'. She thanks M. Kei for his constant support..

Kayla Daley

sparkling tears
on his eyelashes . . .
a summer breeze
from the door
he kept closed for years

~*United States*

Kayla Daley is twenty-two years old and she lives in Hattiesburg, Mississippi, in the United States. She has been recently published in Ribbons Winter Issue 2015: Volume 11, Number 1. At Mississippi State University, she is currently pursuing a degree in Wildlife Biology and her hobbies besides writing tanka and haiku are watching movies with her supportive boyfriend, Chase.

Kath Abela Wilson

windy deck
in the ferried night
an eyelet
pattern the gulls make as a jigsaw
scatters bayside

~Staten Island, New York, USA

immersed overwhelmed
the bridge might flood
all we can do
is stop and listen
to the rain

gilded maple
reddening where you turned
I turn
as if retrospect
could make a different turn

a sort of holly berry
passion you can tell by
his choice of color
the smooth stacked openness
of his love

so the sky too
has bones knitting
above below
night and day in silence
like roots like words

overnight pressed dark
to white stars caught
in the thin green
net of time we're fresh
fallen points

~Pasadena, California, USA

Sunday papers
my heavy bag delivery
New York Times
one long listening stop on the doorstep
of Chopin or Liszt

~Staten Island, New York, USA

bloodstones
scattered the strand snapped
in the crosswalk
my timeless crossings to gather
and protect

~Pasadena, California, USA

inside the peach
after sunset
as real
as the color
of my heart

~Tuscany, Italy

Gifts

礼物

Shanghai, Summer, 2014

Kath Abela Wilson & Yiwei Huang

Yiwei Huang, English-Chinese translator

we return
to the old temple
our meeting place
do you still have the cup
I gave you filled with rain

我们回到
画中的古庙
初次相识的地方
那时我送你的杯子里
是否还盛着露水

the white birds
on our way
to yellow mountain
could you recognize them
here on campus in Shanghai

　　去黄山的路上
　　你我曾看见
　　许多白色的鸟儿
　　在这上海的校园里
　　你认出他们了么

a bell rung
by the river
smooth white stones
are they filled
with wings

　　小河边
　　传来钟声响
　　白色的卵石
　　他们是否
　　收起了翅膀

~Shanghai, China

Kath Abela Wilson is leader of Tanka Poets on Site, and secretary of
the Tanka Society of America. She travels the world with her
mathematician husband Rick Wilson to mathematics conferences. They
perform her new and published poetry in many countries and in the US.
Rick plays flutes of the world, especially the Japanese shakuhachi
during her tanka performances. They will perform at TankaSunday, in
Albany, NY, in 2015. Kath Abela interviews poets and creates a weekly
Poetry Corner for the online ColoradoBlvd.net, presenting tanka to a
larger audience.

Yiwei Huang is a Lecturer at China Pharmaceutical University in
Nanjing, China. He studied at Nanyang Technological University, and
earned his PhD in combinatorics in Singapore. He has a wife and one
small daughter. His website celebrates his poetic process and his
collaborations with his friends in the US, https://
huangyiwei.wordpress.com. He has collaborated with Kath Abela
Wilson in performances in China and during his first trip to the US in
2013.

Ken Slaughter

fireworks
after sundown
on Labor Day
our laid-off neighbor
yells at his cat

seeing me
dripping wet
and worried
my therapist recommends
a bigger umbrella

Steppenwolf
lurking on the Kindle
I stir
half and half
into my dark roast

she sprawls out
over my lap
and purrs
only an animal
and yet . . .

~Grafton, Massachusetts, USA

stumbling
into the bathroom
I bump my knee . . .
that hunt in the dark
for dad's urinal

~Cincinnati, Ohio, USA

Ken Slaughter discovered tanka in 2011. In 2012 he won second prize
and an honorable mention in the TSA international contest. His tanka
have been published in many online and print journals. Ken lives in
Massachusetts with his wife and two cats. He maintains a website to
help tanka writers keep track of submission deadlines: All Things
Tanka.

Larry Kimmel

things
that flower
seek
the light
at all costs

a nature poet?
really?   where are
the black flies
the nettles
the humidity?

countless syllables
and still
and still
I've not explained
myself

in the park
under a sky
by Monet,
the girl
in the strawberry dress

OCD
let's put it this way—
I've read *War and Peace*
three times,
once

cherita

Larry Kimmel

along this street

of yellow leaves and berries red,
a sudden telephone—and

justlikethat!
nameless fear
is afoot

midnight

in the palm of the coleus leaf
a heart the color of dark blood

and
the telephone,
silent

in a vacant lot

in snowsuits, turning bodywise
to communicate

three kids
become
astronauts

Trailways Bus Depot

*". . . but a guy with one of your
costumes said . . ."*

*"we call them
uniforms,
ma'am"*

winter

all over Amherst
dogs are wearing snappy sweaters

they take
their employees
for walks

out of the blue

and without a word
she packed and left—

the locusts were buzzing
and the old dog laid
in the dusty drive

sedoka

Larry Kimmel

cracks of sunlight
through blue curtains,
mourning doves insisting—
just want to quit,
drop
off the map so I can't be found

caught adjusting her bra
she laughs—
for a moment
all's fun and flirty
and then
I am old again

a stone explodes
in the campfire,

overhead
lights of a jet too high to hear—

today on CNN:
3.3 MILLION YEAR OLD GIRL FOUND

~Massachusetts, United States

*Larry Kimmel was born in Johnstown, Pennsylvania. His most recent
books are "this hunger, tissue-thin;" and "shards and dust." He lives
with his wife in the hills of western Massachusetts.*

What To Do With Love

a selection of love tanka

Liam Wilkinson

one day
a nephew, a niece
will look at my poems
and wonder
what kept him so long from love?

love burned
in my throat
all night long
even the moon failed
to smother the flames

each morning
I place a gentle
ear to your chest
eager to hear
the faint engine of love

my old heart
has slackened
around this love
youth's elasticity
a gossamer memory

the kettle boils
the spoon drops
into the cup
I pour
my heart out

gallant, charging
stillness
where my heart used to be
love unveils
an equestrian statue

our first tentative steps
along the stepping
stones of love
we hardly made a ripple
on this tossed and turned tide

learning
one another
suddenly
this lifelong fluency
in you

seeing heart shapes
in everything
these old chipped marbles
I call
my eyes

a few months
into our love
all my words
the shape
of your mouth

my first gift to you
*The Collected Poems
of Seamus Heaney*
it too wears the creases
of a long, long time

the church where we were married
now in other hands
other beliefs
after all
love is the only persuasion

what is it about love?
in each window
the jolting
shock
of the same old sky

your gaze
holds me
like a scratched LP
all my imperfections
filled with faint melody

now that I'm covered
in years of self-loathing
what shapes
do your eyes
feel out of me?

submerged in grief
your skin
softens and glows
this cruel wish
to savour your sadness

in a purple hand
an old love letter
from the young
fool
who became my wife

glancing into the gorge
of what cold have been
my stomach turns
I dash through the house
scattering your pet names

clutching at pens
I never knew
what to do with love
now, sick with distance,
words charge into lines

~England

long cold river

Liam Wilkinson & *Joy McCall*

at moonrise
I hear
all my selves
waking
within me

> *I dream*
> *at the setting*
> *of the moon*
> *of mountain minnows*
> *and a long cold river*

a sliver of moon
remains
I toss the stone
of my soul
into dark brackish water

specks of dreams

Liam Wilkinson & *Joy McCall*

under a rough
draft of day
I stand at the sink
splashing, splashing
specks of dreams

> *scattered*
> *splinters of bone*
> *under my feet*
> *the nightmare replays*
> *the needle stuck*

into the inkwell
a nib, a finger,
a whole self
broken into
five lines of memory

landlocked dreams

Liam Wilkinson & *Joy McCall*

landlocked dreams
salty with desire
he makes a tall ship
of his writing desk
and rigs it with five lines

> *the poet*
> *yearns for the sea*
> *for the sound*
> *of waves, endlessly*
> *washing on the shore*

a lucky seashell
in his palms
rolling, rolling
he pierces the moon
with a bowsprit pen

~England / *England*

Liam Wilkinson's poetry has appeared in such journals as Modern English Tanka, Presence, Paper Wasp, Atlas Poetica, Simply Haiku, Bottle Rockets, Skylark, Lynx and many others. He has served as editor of Prune Juice, 3LIGHTS and Modern Haiga. He lives in North Yorkshire, England, and his website can be found at ldwilkinson.blogspot.co.uk

Joy McCall is a nurse/counsellor, retired because of paraplegia following a motorcycle crash. She has written all kinds of poetry for 50 years, publishing occasionally here and there. She lives on the edge of the old walled city of Norwich, England, having spent much of her life in Canada. She treasures most her loved ones, nature, books, words and tattoos, life, and poetry. Keibooks published her 'circling smoke, scattered bones', 'hedgerows' and 'rising mist, fieldstones'. She thanks M. Kei for his constant support..

Double Tanka

Liam Wilkinson

collected poems

a bare beech
reaches
to write
moss-green lines
on the sky

my fingers
fumble
inside an old typer
looking
for lost verses

a new light

her love
is self-serving
she wishes
to see me
in a new light

morning after
the eclipse
a new light
repaints
my shadow

metrophobia

bold edges
sharp corners
the metropolis
writes its lines
all over you

bullied
by an old self
your heart
a smear
on your sleeve

hour of vespers

echoing
through the village
giggles
fast footsteps
and willow bark horns

dressed in leaves
and a wickerwork hat
Jack In The Green
drags his shadow
to the well

green man

from the stubbiest
pencil point
a gnarled line
of old selves
and ancient roots

I glance in the mirror
to watch
brambles rambling
from the dark
of mouth and nostril

some other depth
remembering Ted

reading your lines
suddenly
your voice inside me
papering my throat
carpeting my tongue

death is
a noisy silence
I tear open a memory
for its thousands
of giggling pips

elegy
for JWB

what to do
with the memory
of your hands
your glasses
your dry, silent laugh

a magpie
chisels the breeze
this autumn dawn
my grief thins
to a fine pencil point

cusp

teal blue dawn
a trapped linnet
singing
into the mechanism
of a Remington Rand

and what is it
I'm looking for
I wonder
picking up my luck
rattling it, shaking it

another place

out of sea wind
and silence
I sculpt
the statues
of all my selves

another place
I stare out
to sea
with the eyes
of a hundred men

hope street

childhood in
rags around
each iron flourish
a clenched
nostalgia

rain
in paradise
the city
erupts
with copper cormorants

nocturne

across the dark fields
a jagged line
the midnight fox
screams
down the moon

always night
in my head
the gibbous moon
and I
wear our darkness well

inheritance

what mum used to call
resting her eyes
now I know
the weight of the worry
behind them

coursing through
my blood
kindness and anxiety
this root-cracked path
I follow

a mellow song

the teal typewriter
sings
a mellow song
my head and heart
are miles apart

this simple innocence
unsexed
within me
I carry the weight
of my lightness

dramatis personae

a soft
simulated
sunrise
in the grand theatre
of my imagination

flocking
towards a big idea
throngs
of old selves
and parts I'm playing

shards

afternoon dream
smashed to
smithereens
I bloody these hands
to salvage an old self

counting coins
on the kitchen table
she wakes me
dreams
webbing my fingers

first of spring

am I flirting
with a hope
I can't hold?
rain mingles
with snow

snow mingles
with rain
pulling
my selves
together

folds and creases

blue Saturday
skies stretched
across the bonnet
I unfold the map
of another weekend

another week
I put on
my taut creases
my faded hopes
and jeans

esplanade

the shark
of this cold
winter day
tastes me
and discards me

biting wind
limbs and lines
scattered
along the coast
I chase my pages

stones

tomorrow
feeds itself fat
in my mind
so many stones
of anxiety

from the edge
of a cliff
I hurl my heart
into the tide's
chest of drawers

breeze

and after tomorrow
what then
the door opens slightly
but no breeze
enters

writing
collaborations
with an old self
this first green day
of spring

north riding
for Diane

strained conversations
of ancient elms
along the roadside
crows peck
exclamations in the mist

blanketing the bell heather
a cracked and peeling
map of mythology
here be dragons
scrawled in moorland mud

consolation

the still black dawn
is pierced
with a tiny white light
we shuffle across the lawn
in search of a gate

slow launch
of my wonder
you arch your neck
to catch a glimpse
of my wandering mind

hot air

lowering a spyglass
over my lines
I inflate
the hot air balloon
of my letter to you

let us meet
I write
wondering how
to live up to my lies
and magnifications

the pouring floor

white hot
dreams
trickling into mind
old fires
and old flames

I wake in the shape
of a clenched fist
every inch of me
cast
in the bronze of night

night lights

flickering bulb
of my night light
I dare not dream
the path to sleep
is strewn with shadows

under pink ribbons of dawn
a Beethoven sonata
I glance at the moon
still there
after all these years

expedition

old poems
in old notebooks
little fossils
that prove
I once existed

looking for
a way out of
writer's block
I ask myself
for directions

first draft

these faces
on the morning bus
crumpled
like
aborted stories

I guess
we were all
good ideas
once
upon a time

to my job

I give so much of myself
to my job
every memory
of whom
I once was

a phone call
to my boss
I'm too tired
to chisel another corner
off my ambitions

dreamscapes

old seaside town
dressed in silver night
holidaymakers dreaming
the dreamscapes
I once drew

just a lonely insomniac
spinning a lasso
on the beach
I try to tie my worries
around the waning moon

vacancies

early
Sunday morning
sirens
I slam my fist
down on the city

spire to spire
I cast
a vacant stare
all my old beliefs
godless, gone

two sculptures

so alive
this Frink
I wonder
which of us
is the sculpture

in the gallery
for two hours
I stare
at the sculpture
on a vacant plinth

this quiet disquiet

full moon
floats
in a winter fog
each worry wears
a coat of moss

full moon
tilts
its gentle head
once, you wore
the darkness well

all I know

for Sanford

as I pattern this table
with coffee cup rings
I think of you
spilling your tanka
on the other side of the world

cheers
I say
tipping the ocean
sipping the spume
toasting you for all I know

the right words

for Joy

under the electric blanket
of blue dusk
I dismantle my vocabulary
in search of
the right words

dear poet
you write a wire
down my spine
and ink
a thousand volts along it

~United Kingdom

Liam Wilkinson's poetry has appeared in such journals as Modern English Tanka, Presence, Paper Wasp, Atlas Poetica, Simply Haiku, Bottle Rockets, Skylark, Lynx and many others. He has served as editor of Prune Juice, 3LIGHTS and Modern Haiga. He lives in North Yorkshire, England and his website can be found at ldwilkinson.blogspot.co.uk.

His Busy Heart

M. Kei

the hawk wind
blows very cold
this November—
I think of him up north
and try to keep myself warm

moving again
I want to settle down
and find a place
where my arthritic hip
can live in peace

always attracted to
unavailable men,
when will I find
one who will fit me
into his busy heart?

~United States

What Love Can Do

M. Kei

I am in your city
to be sold,
but I have a heart
made of vulture bones
and old ashes

Let us try what love can do. *

* "Let us try what love can do."—William Penn

M. Kei

moments of a day,
sifted, sorted, discarded,
by a careless hand
on a stony beach
in spring

a pair
of wild turkey hens
strolling
along a
country lane

words stacked
like cans
hoarded
against the day
of scarcity

that neighbor
with his ambitions,
unaware
I have named his concrete lions
Xerxes and Darius

turning off
the music to
better hear
the crack and rumble
of a summer storm

the persistent growl
of thunder at
the periphery of sleep;
a night of flickering
uneasy dreams

her thong
and micro-mini
in the laundry—
unwelcome proof
my daughter is grown

pretending
once again
to like it when
my daughter fixes
coq au vin

I'm not lonely
sailing the cold grey sea
I'm only lonely
when I'm with
other people

the lateen mizzen
an isosceles right triangle
laid out
on the floor of the sail loft
waiting for the sailmaker's needle

what more
does a man want?
hard work,
pleasant quarters,
amiable shipmates

the forepeak
as dim and full
as a barn,
coils of ropes instead
of smoked hams hanging

the ship's cat and I
sharing a bunk at midnight
both awake
listening to the howling
of a winter gale

hauling the sternfall
with the mate in the Zodiac,
remembering when
my back wouldn't even
let me lift a plate

'the shrew'
they called my grandmother
a veteran of war
no one ever suggested
a mere woman had PTSD

grandma
was a veteran
the red of her
coffin flag still crimson
after all these years

the tide flows
easily to the sea and
just as easily returns—
if only it were so
with the human heart

a little faster now—
the tide picks up
the pace
it rushes to the sea
and leaves behind the city

~Maryland, USA

M. Kei is a tall ship sailor and award-winning poet who lives on
Maryland's Eastern shore. He is the editor of Atlas Poetica : A
Journal of World Tanka. He was the editor-in-chief of Take Five :
Best Contemporary Tanka, Vols. 1–4, and the editor of Bright Stars,
An Organic Tanka Anthology. His most recent collection of poetry is
January, A Tanka Diary (2013). He is also the author of the award-
winning gay Age of Sail adventure novels, Pirates of the Narrow Seas
(blogspot.narrowseas.com). He can be followed on Twitter
@kujakupoet, or visit AtlasPoetica.org.

friend

Maggie Gladding

the waves
lap against your feet
the sand
is a cushion for you
gulls cry in a dark grey sky

on the docks
a few visitors stand
the others
have left for fear
of the thunderstorm

you seem
to be alone
both
in your thoughts
and on the shore

thunder roars
lightning crackles
you turn and see
the remaining tourists
flee for shelter

slowly
with your shoulders drooping
you stand
you feel a heaviness
overwhelm you

you drag your feet
along the water's edge
the downpour starts
a shard of lightning
slashes the sky

a grey shape
runs towards you, you stumble . . .
a tongue caresses your cheek
you stand, thanking the dog,
man's best friend

~*Lexington, Kentucky, USA*

Maggie Gladding (age 11) lives in Lexington, Kentucky. She enjoys writing, singing, acting, gardening and spending time with friends. Her blood family and heart family on both sides of the pond deeply shape who she is.

Note: Minors must have their work submitted by an adult agent when contributing to Atlas Poetica. We do not accept unagented submissions from minors less than 16 years of age.

Winter Days

Marilyn Humbert

Polished glass windows set in stark white walls come into view as I round the bend to the nursing home. Mother no longer greets me with the smile of recognition, but sits stoic, blanket wrapped in a rocker with that faraway look.

pink petals pool
beneath the vase—
my mother
dreams of Lucy-doll
skipping and hopscotch

Our conversation is one sided. I tell her about my children and grandchildren. Every so often she asks 'who are you dear?'
Time moves slowly, I keep checking my watch.

winter winds
sweep snow-bound plains—
my goodbye kiss
fills your eyes with fear,
black-smudges smear the sky

~*Bendigo, Victoria, Australia*

Treasures

Marilyn Humbert

July, dry season in Central Australia. Coiled around afternoon shadows, a chill wind gnaws at our exposed faces. Yulara campground is bustling. Caravans, camper trailers, tents, adults and kids all jostle for a spot to camp. We pitch our tent on a small grassy knoll, back from the red-dust road.

outback . . .
stunted scrub bows
to the west wind
following ancient trails
carved into the landscape

Night falls suddenly with no twilight as stars glint against the ink-black sky. The wind drives campers to their shelters and the campground falls silent early. A dingo howls near the perimeter fence and another howl answers in the distance, their voices sing in age-old ritual.

mid-winter
the southern cross
is a beacon . . .
light flooding the night sky
Uluru and dingo trails

The gusty wind shakes the tent. My sleep is disturbed by icy draughts and dusty images. Shadows flicker with moonshine ebb and flow. In the morning we crawl from our hike tent.

gleaming
in the weak morn sun
white frost—
stars from heaven
glitter about my feet

~*Yulara campground near Uluru Northern Territory, Australia*

Burning

Marilyn Humbert

Morning mist dissolves revealing lucerne thick with fists of purple flowers. In afternoon sunshine he hitches the mower to the tractor. The years of dust and drought fade.

Clouds bob above the tree line as he rakes the cut into neat windrows running the length of the paddock. He leaves them to dry for three or four days before baling and storing under cover. This curing reduces moisture content and risk of spontaneous combustion.

Around this time I sense something is wrong.

this tightness
at the base of my throat
numbness spreads
the doctor's
monotone diagnosis

My treatment starts immediately.

no choice
radiation burns deep
the price
changes my body
scars my mind

Four weeks after stacking the bales, the haystack is lost.

~Calivil, Victoria, Australia

Note: Each year a number of bale haystacks are destroyed in Australia due to spontaneous combustion.

Son of Mine

Marilyn Humbert

a tapestry of stars
reflected
in the still pool
I dream of a child
not yet born

beside you
I hold my breath
release your hand . . .
and delight
in your first steps

school days
friends
learning—
this new thing
your own ideas

who is right
am I wrong . . . .
my confusion
as you choose
a different life

in the sun
you stand tall
splendid
in white kufi and thawb
beside your bride

moon and stars
reflected
in the still pool
memories of a child
full grown

~Sydney NSW Australia

Echo Through Time

Marilyn Humbert & Andrew Howe

by the cross
half-buried in mud
a red rosebud
trampled beneath
alien feet

    solemn hands
    mound mudstone
    excavating
    brilliant white stones
    parade across the field

in shadow
standing by the portal
to another time
silver soldiers
polished to a mirror shine

    pegged rope
    grids the trench
    east to west
    tarnished buttons
    line frayed fabric

on an endless plain
they salute and march
through the gate
a cold-hearted wind
accompanies battle songs

    musical staves
    scrawl paper fragments
    click . . .
    bayonets fixed
    'it's a long way to Tipperary'

orders acid-etched
on copper ribbons
fast-tracked
by cosmic couriers
through the nebula

    silent faces
    dashed by rain
    await
    twilight bulges
    and the evening star

only gods
of space and time
hear death poems—
soldiers resting
under winter's grass

~Australia

Marilyn Humbert lives in the Northern suburbs of Sydney, NSW, surrounded by bush. Her pastimes include writing free verse, tanka, haiku and related genre. Her tanka and haiku can be found in Australian and overseas journal and anthologies. Some of her free verse poems have been published and awarded prizes in competitions. She is the leader of the Bottlebrush tanka group and a member of Tanka Huddle and Bowerbird.

Andrew Howe is an Australian naval officer who lives in NSW. His interests include military history, geology, and reading and writing tanka.

Marilyn Morgan

early morning
the sky's on fire
deer
foraging for food
snow to their bellies

about the bear
in my bedroom
last night . . .
the shutter banging
against the open window

cell phones
dueling
for attention
around the dinner table
gourmet food and fine wine

late October
trees weeping
leaves . . .
the road ahead
long, cold and dark

early spring
walking in the woods
sun slips through the trees
onto the path . . .
look, trout lilies blooming

mallard and his woman
didn't return this spring
strange
what we miss
in life

snow falling
on the daffodils
their long faces
drooping
to the ground

lonely . . .
cries
of gulls
across the river
early in the morning

a winter moon
tonite
I remember
skiing thru the woods
trees talking in the cold

my granddaughters
skiing
scarves and hair
tangling
       in the wind

~*United States*

Marilyn Morgan is a retired English teacher. She lives and writes in New Hartford, New York, USA. Her poems have been published in Atlas Poetica, Bright Stars, Ribbons, A Hundred Gourds, American Tanka, and others.

Our First Dance

Marsha Oseas

We double dated to our senior year Homecoming Dance, you with my best friend and I with yours, a star of the football team. My date was one of the school's finest athletes, lettering in football and gymnastics. There was a picture of him in the school yearbook doing the iron cross on the still rings, muscles bulging but face relaxed. The next year, a car accident rendered him quadriplegic. Eventually, former muscles atrophied and he became a Raggedy Andy version of himself, his massive head too big for his fragile neck to hold.

I dreaded the dancing to begin because I didn't want to watch you dance with her. I danced a slow dance with my date, the football star. He was huge, nervous and sweaty, and we were both uncomfortable and awkward.

Towards the end of the evening you asked me to dance. We fit together perfectly. In your arms I felt exactly right. You held me closely, our joined hands resting on your chest. We just swayed to the music. Inside I was twirling, swirling, whirling, light-headed but trying to hide it, heart beating too fast, moist in unexpected places. It was thrilling. I could feel your breath on my temple. I was ecstatic and remember hoping no one would notice.

When the dance was over, you went back to my friend and I to my date. But everything, everything was different.

> the dervish whirls
> himself into oblivion
> tsunami strengthens
> slamming, smashing, destroying
> no one left to salvage

~Los Angeles, California, USA

The Kiss

Marsha Oseas

Having reunited after one of our more lengthy separations, we had just rented a house in Hollywood, California. It was a little guest house behind the landlord's bigger house in front. You, me and our cat, Ethan. Neither of us was working yet. I had never been to California. I was deliriously happy to be with you, to be in a new city, to be on vacation. The house was cute. We wallpapered the kitchen in a pattern that delighted me. I liked it so much, we used the same at our next house, but in a different color. Ethan the cat loved it too. One day I heard Joe, the landlord, saying to someone, "I didn't know you liked bananas!" It turns out he was speaking to Ethan, who daily showed up on Joe's porch and was invited in for a visit.

One sunny afternoon, waiting at a stoplight for the "walk" signal, we kissed. It was not an inappropriate kiss for waiting on a corner. It was a sweet kiss, tender, sincere and intimate. A man approached us holding out a five dollar bill. He asked us to take the money. He said that watching our kiss "made his day." We were always great kissers.

> we stopped for a kiss
> tender, delicate, ardent
> your hand on my cheek
> eyes open, fondly gazing
> each of us lost in our love

~Los Angeles, California, USA

Grandma Fanny

Marsha Oseas

I was the eldest child of Grandma Fanny's favorite son.

She cooked. That's what she did, and what a fantastic cook she was. Her kosher pickles sizzled when you bit into them. If she made a cake for company and I came early, she would cut me a piece and serve it later with Marsha's piece missing. When people asked what happened to the cake, she would wink at me. The phyllo dough for cherry strudel rolled out over the entire dining room table was so sheer the pattern of the tablecloth showed through. I slept on a Murphy-in-a-door bed when I spent the night.

When she was alive, extended family gathered there for holidays. After, no one would do the work.

She died from breast cancer, her arm and hand swollen huge like a ham hock. No one ever told me why. Later, I had it too.

> I belong to you
> you give me grandma kisses
> your eyes shine, loving
> healing me from mama spite
>   (or is it mama's bite?)
> you're gone. where's my safe place now?

~*Los Angeles, California, USA*

What My Mother Taught Me

Marsha Oseas

My mother didn't teach me to cook, or clean, or how to ride a bus, or write a check, or the basics of good hygiene. She didn't mention the meaning of life, the importance of family, or how to live with integrity. She did teach me something invaluable, though, which I pass along to you:

"Don't eat the yellow snow"

At the age of 5 or 6, I was hiding alone behind a garage spying on a few of the older boys playing in the snowy field behind our houses. What were they doing? They were laughing, and holding their hands between their legs, looking down at the snow and laughing some more. After they left, I went to see if I could discover what all the laughing was about. I saw what appeared to be writing in the snow. It was kind of squiggly. This must be the yellow snow my mother was talking about.

I wanted to write something too, but couldn't figure out how. I was disappointed. Much, much later, many years later, a light bulb moment—oh, the envy.

> an ice ball barrage
> keeps snow forts secure from girls
> in the snowy field
> boys write messages in code
> with mysterious pencils

~*United States*

Marsha Oseas

so sorry, mommy
I'm from another planet
impossible child
I don't think like earthlings do
there's no way you can know me

we spent a lifetime
but you never got my jokes
I'm a funny girl
we lived without the laughter
no wonder we didn't last

~*Los Angeles, California, USA*

After spending the better part of four decades working in law firms and later for the government where the writing offended her with its purposeful verbosity and incomprehensibility, Marsha Oseas is relieved to be writing tanka.

Marshall Bood

two teenagers smoking
on the stoop
of the house declared
Unsanitary and Unfit
for Occupation

bus shelter advert
peeled off . . .
an empty bottle
of Listerine
left open

a one-armed homeless man
holds dirty jeans up
styrofoam cup clenched
in his mouth
waiting

everyone drawn
to the lights
of 7–11—
moths or near-
death experiences

~*Canada*

Marshall Bood lives in Regina, Saskatchewan, Canada. He visits his Mom and her rescue dog in Carlyle, SK.

Reading Neruda,
A Ryuka Rensaku

Matsukaze

on a cool evening
as always, at your home
seated at your desk
making ryuka

no rules
no strings attached
just raw, good-time sex
with the man i love

i find i am aroused
by anything
such as the way your slip
hangs from your shoulders

a lacquer rice bowl
a small gift
from the married-one
on his return from Japan

stranded in the rain
in front of the city library
a warm memory
of us reading Neruda

there's a part of me
that desires to be known
worldwide for something . . .
not sure what, but something

in as few syllables as possible
i often distill
my daily happenings
within my diary

the rise of her breasts
full and youthful
this is my third visit
to her home

again, alone in this house
listening to Shirley Horn
the rustle of
dry branches outside

damp grass and peeling paint
this old cottage
is still quaint
even after his passing

a full hotel this evening
a young man
asks me
for detergent to wash

ready for soul food
the house smells
of cooking stew—
repose feels good

'my love is for sale . . .'
some sultry chanteuse croons
please give me another
glass of oblivion

for creating plant life
some compost made up of egg shells—
another batch of his clothing
to be washed

met in the music studio
within fifteen minutes
recording some ballad—
a Monday rainfall

while washing dishes
i come to the conclusion
that i am not
as clever as you suppose

all throughout this business meeting
scribbling
ryuka after ryuka—
damn! i need a vacation

black-power, my man
is the sound of your loud fingers
carving whispers
along my woman-thighs

a night of passion
you stand behind me on the verandah
your hands, comfortable on my hips;
you, in my life

mid-year fasting . . .
reading several passages
from the Torah
does the One-G-d hear me?

he prefers a high-brow lover
but alas, i am
colloquial in my mannerisms
—early bus to Cameron

Holiday Inn Express—
arriving after 1 am
it often feels
like i'm in another world

over oysters
telling a dear brother:
'you do not lack faith just because
you must see a psychiatrist.'

another night
of spilling ryuka
with whatever words
well up within me

from this Muslim brother
received tulips
and a few senryu
—a student i'd been teaching

yet again
here is another genre
of oriental poetry that i
might make my mark in

tonight's reading
Psalm 119.
a kind guests brings me
dinner from Taco Bell

to appease him
i dress in next-to-nothing
and sashay around the room
singing the blues

watching through the partially opened door
my daughter
pads her bra
striving to look older

early this morning
treading fallen leaves
i find in myself
a bitter heart

misty memories—
within two hours
we'll be heading to the local fair
—my childhood revisited

from the trash i burn
staring into the flames
the image of my father
i see in myself

wallet in hand
i stand in line
waiting patiently
to cash this check

i stand in line
and slowly i lose my resolve
will i return to a man
who doesn't love me?

to hide my tears
i hastily don the hat
i purchased
for my trip to Palm Springs

three weeks have passed,
and at this moment
i realize
how much time i've lost

after ten years
and i still cannot bring myself
to call my mother's home
my own

my family's home,
a pit of lies
of cold shoulders and even colder stares—
the figs have ripened

brushing shoulders
with an aged woman who comes
i give her my place
in line

within my ancestral line
there is a bitterness
that has made
every woman barren, i often think

the young man
has taken his sexuality,
wrapped it in thick brown blankets
and buried it beneath stone

spoke to this young brother on the bus
he tells me he is
banished
to a desert land, an unfeeling place

millions of eyes
document the fury of
protesters
moving fire-like through Baltimore

through a foggy London-town
sunspill on the ground
shall we stop off
at the local pub?

"budding plums
and cooking sweet potatoes
hold my joy"
grandmother tells me

catching sight of grandmother
cutting a step
to some ragtime
by Joplin

quiet rainy day—
peeling potatoes
in a house that no longer
cares for me

the black girl next door
fell for a Japanese man
she's taken up
learning the koto

a swift morning wind
this Wednesday
quickly heading downtown
for a doctor's appointment

an impromptu performance
of a Gershwin standard
at some
dinner club

settling back
enjoying a fresh cup of coffee
on the table
several books of tanka and senryu

finally home
she sits on the edge of the bed
peeling off her stockings
in the semidarkness

after a hard day
soaking in the tub
while he reads me
ryuka of Onna Nabe

come tomorrow
a colleague and i
will Skype
planning this recital

even Emperor Akihito
took a turn
at composing
Okinawan ryuka

on the backs
of indentured slaves
a whole plantation was built
complete with artificial pond

~*United States*

colors

Matsukaze & *Murasame*

finding a moment
to whisper
any and everything
into the ears
of a cluster of grapes

    swearing
    at may-tree thorns
    caught in my hair
    trickle of blood
    down one pale cheek

it is while reading your letters
that i experience life
without fear
and i'm amazed
at all of its colors

    give me
    the brown of earth
    of tree bark
    of your skin and eyes
    and add the blaze of fire

there is
an elusive scent
of honeysuckle
in the pores of your ivory skin
in the womb of words you send

~United States / *England*

Matsukaze
resides in Louisiana
a classical vocalist and actor
a lover of Japanese poetic forms

Murasame
lives in Norwich, England,
growing older
and not much wiser

Mira N. Mataric

sometimes
not doing
just being
is the best for us
and the universe

seems nature is calm
but underneath it all
each cell is active
creating more life
survival is a strife

the stars in the skies
are only a memory
of the dead and long gone
yes only a memory
and the glory of the past

I am a stone
in me murmur
of water
and the time past
I will last

stone
is made
of water
time and
persistence

~United States

Mirjana (Mira) N. Mataric has published 37 books (in English and Serbian) of poetry, short stories, memoirs, and novels, an anthology and several books of translations. Awarded numerous international awards, she has 50 years of active teaching English, Special Education, Russian and Continuing Education. She still teaches Creative Writing and promotes poetry, esp. haiku and tanka, with an "excuse" that it teaches precise, concise and poetic style useful for good prose. Mira organizes and participates in public poetry readings in California and abroad.

Peter Fiore

the widow's tangled hair
her heart tangled between two loves . . .
in the season of flaming maples
she asks me
to brush it out

I hear it
in the rain
like lovers
who though half asleep
wake up intimate

autumn verging on winter
another death in the family
mom and dad peer down a road
indifferent and dark—
you and I too

the blackbird
rides
the currents
thru a hurricane
of white blossoms

I imagine your boots
tangled on the floor
with mine
knowing you'll never love me
again

in the morning
we ate apples and cheese
by the river
my children and me
voices rattling like kites

~United States

The Faithful Husband's Complaint

Peter Fiore

now he has an abscess

makes the left side of his face bulge like a medieval punishment festering in his jaw

he can feel its pressure down the middle of his back when it enflames

his wife says

"well at least you'll be safe I can be sure no woman'll look at you this week with loving eyes."

~United States

Peter Fiore lives and writes in Mahopac, New York, USA. His poems have been published in American Poetry Review, Rattle, Atlas Poetica, Bright Stars, Ribbons, A Hundred Gourds and others. In 2009 Peter published "text messages", the first volume of American Gogyohka poetry. In June 2015, Keibooks published "flowers to the torch", Peter's book of tanka prose.

Rebecca Drouilhet

the fire in the stones
passed from mother to daughter
for generations . . .
a glimpse of the goddess
as I slip the ring on my finger

pressed between
the pages of my life
those nights
we spent beneath the moon
when all the stars were ours

some summer evenings
I think I see your ghost . . .
a fog
drifting in from the sea,
a sailor searching for home

~United States

Rebecca Drouilhet is a retired registered nurse whose haiku and tanka have appeared in numerous print journals and e-zines. She and her husband have written a book of haiku titled Lighting a Path. She lives in Picayune, Mississippi where she enjoys reading, playing word games and spending time with her large family.

tanrenga

Robert Epstein & *Joy McCall*

still-dark morning
I ask Jesus
for a light
the woods catch fire
blazing all day

therapy office
a wasp on the window
wants out
like these uttered dreams
in the end, it dies

stepping out
but not too far
Ides of March
changing my mind
risking . . . everything

~United States / *England*

Robert Epstein, a psychotherapist by training, lives and works in the San Francisco Bay Area. He has edited five haiku anthologies and his own books of haiku include: A Walk Around Spring Lake; Checkout Time is Noon; and Haiku Forest Afterlife.

Joy McCall is a nurse/counsellor, retired because of paraplegia following a motorcycle crash. She has written all kinds of poetry for 50 years, publishing occasionally here and there. She lives on the edge of the old walled city of Norwich, England, having spent much of her life in Canada. She treasures most her loved ones, nature, books, words and tattoos, life, and poetry. Keibooks published her 'circling smoke, scattered bones', 'hedgerows' and 'rising mist, fieldstones'. She thanks M. Kei for his constant support.

Ryuka Conversation in Kume Island

Ryoh Honda
Ryoh Honda, Uchinaaguchi Translator

* All ryuka on the left are anonymous and they have their own tunes to be sung.

sirashi haikawani
nagariyuku sakura
sukuti umisatuni
nuchai hakira

Tune: Shirashihaikawa

I shall scoop the petals
of cherry blossoms floating
in Shirashihai river
a wreath for my love

the irritation should be
regarded as freshness
awkward songs of warblers
in early March

tubitachuru habiru
maziyu mati tsirira
hananu mutu wamiya
shiranu amunu

Tune: Nakagushikuhantame

a butterfly flying up
please wait for a moment
accompany me as I
have been so naive

had been chasing blindly
the light only you could see
black wings of swallowtail
scattered on the road

ikutushiyu fitin
niguri nenu munuya
shirashi haikawanu
mizinu kagami

Tune: Shirashihaikawa

no muddiness although
it has passed numerous years
Shirashihai river's
mirror of water

into the depth of my soul
kuusu, aged *awamori*
has penetrated—wandering
lights of firefly

watarariru uchiyu
watararanu funini
nutaru kunu wamidu
mumu ramisharu

Tune: Mutusanyama

to the crossable sea
took the un-crossable boat
only hating my doom
one hundred times

please let me forget
what I need to forget
into the edge of the sea
the sky fading out

ikana yanbarunu
karikiguni yatin
nzotu tai yariba
hananu miyaku

Tune: Jintooyoo

even in the countries of
withered forest, if with you
there will be a capital
of bright flowers

listening to blackly fermenting
awamori mash in tank
the silent sound concealing
ocean tempest

kuminu guyunu matsi
shichaidanu makura
umiwarabi nzoya
wa udi makura

Tune: Kumihantame

the Kume's five-leaves-pine
crawling branches as pillows
you the loveliest love
my arm as a pillow

cores of pine, towards the sky
growing and punching holes
the blue of young summer
drawn to the ground

sayaka tiru tsichini
sasuwcriti waminu
nagamïran tumuti
njïti icʁun

Tune: Nakagushikuhantame

invited by shining moon
I'm just going outside
to find somewhere else
for looking it up

taking a long look at
islands on the southern
horizon—buttons of
the sky and the sea

~Japan

Ryoh Honda is a kajin (tanka poet) in Tokyo, Japan. Enjoying tanka practice, he publishes his works, tanka reviews and essays in some journals occasionally.

old stuff

Sanford Goldstein

want
to hear some old
records,
I've forgotten
how the long-gone males sing

over
the hills far beyond lies
an unknown land,
the usual coward in me
hesitates again and again

tell myself
the end is near and I face
that empty curtain,
take me, fling me off again
into undiscovered countries

I look up
during my illness and the clock
says four,
how well I know my Japanese
that four means death

destiny
faces me tomorrow
and tomorrow,
will my fears not curl
in three separate places?

hot
as the devil
outside,
cold as a freezer inside
and I tremble waiting

~Japan

Sanford Goldstein still lives in Japan. He will be 90 at the end of the year. He still continues to write tanka and to submit to various journals.

Sandi Pray

a wet wind
tears at my hair . . .
leaving you
for another storm
just like my father

tapping a feather
against my lips . . .
now and then
i think about
being in love

shades of rose . . .
the sound of a palm
at sunset
searching the horizon
for one more beer

does it matter
which way i go?
rising early
turkey tracks everywhere
in the sand

happiness
without reason
on a spring night
i sit with the forest
listening to green

shivering
at a butterfly's touch
once again
i am found, praying
to your lilacs

as far as
my eyes will take me
i follow
the sound of blue
out to sea

ripples . . .
the rise and fall
of a lotus
my young-self's wings
much smoother now

far from home
beach-deep in awesome
the waves
i used to ride
still rolling on

moss hanging
into a bayou's
stillness . . .
thinking of the comet
i used to be

one by one
you go away . . .
what remains
of owls and memories
i finish alone

a meteorite
came my way
tonight
i'm an easy drunk
for any star

daffodils bloom
in the old cat's ashes
quietly
a new year has come
knocking at my heart

storm warning
as the cat in my lap
begins to purr
i listen to anger
shaped like sky

a face
passing through clouds
on the pond
how strange i always seem
to myself

i wear
rose colored glasses
you say . . .
smiling i take your hand
with rainbows in my eyes

at the edge
of the gravestone
two cracks down
where spring will bloom
a dandelion

to and fro
the way of a moth
in lamplight . . .
i'm not sure what
i'd do with wings

winter rain . . .
the garden is
so lonely
without you,
bumblebee

a plastic heart
with white ribbons . . .
outside the ER
in a spring breeze
the sound of crows

~United States

*Sandi Pray is a retired high school media specialist living in the wilds of
the North Carolina mountains and forest marshes of North Florida.
Living a vegan life, she is an avid hiker and lover of all critters.*

Susan Burch

before
using abreva
on my cold sore
I kiss him
good-bye

missing
from these journals
my voice
no words left
to speak of this grief

handmade kite
all the hours spent crafting
your dance with the sky—
I bet no one ever told you
you were a mistake

the pink azaleas
he places by my bedside
look like spring—
I inhale the newest scent
guilt with hints of neglect

meeting her at the top
of the Empire State Building—
what he won't do
that makes her question
is he "the one" . . .

a year
without an invitation
to his tanka group—
at ventriloquist practice
I throw my voice   away

knowing you're gone
he sleeps every night
atop your tombstone
your dog, now ours
except those missing hours

bad enough
she was mom's favorite
as a child
her son takes after my dad
the spitting image

still waiting
two hours after school
to be picked up
she stares at her shoes
untied again

inviting me in
my widowed neighbor tells me
about her husband
how good he was in bed
after he died

your heaped words
of mushy gushy praise
make me sick
the stink
of insincerity

~Hagerstown, Maryland, USA

Susan Burch resides in Hagerstown, Maryland, with her husband, 2 kids, and warped sense of humor. She loves reading, doing puzzles, and Coca-Cola Slurpees.

Susan King

who means more
him
or the cat?
I have to say
it's a close-run thing

talking to myself . . .
it's a pity
I have nothing
of interest
to say

her news
can't be good
yet again
she's splashed out
on high-fashion boots

does he care
how tough times are
this banker
with his cuff links
of monogrammed gold?

any death
is still a death
swatting
into oblivion
an out-of-season fly

rain-shiny roof tiles
a mother-of-pearl sky
all is not lost
even
on this downbeat day

Susan King lives in North Wales, United Kingdom. She has been writing haiku since 2002 and has now decided to "spread her poetic wings" and try her hand at tanka.

Three Related Tanka

Tim Callahan

the brain
may think
it runs the show
the bladder
calls the shots

I thought
today that I'd
sleep in
my cats
had other plans

I can bend down
and touch
my toes
the problem's
standing up again

~United States

Tim Callahan is an artist who worked for many years in the animation industry. He had written some poetry since he was in his thirties, but didn't start writing poetry in earnest until he was was in his middle sixties. He is a published author and a regular contributor to Skeptic Magazine. He lives with his wife, Bonnie, in the foothills of the Angeles National Forest and often hikes on trails in the foothills.

what matters

Tony Beyer & *Joy McCall*

at either end
of the earth
spring and autumn
the best times
to sow new grass

hard black seeds
falling on the ground
spring rains
the morning glory
is born again

strange fate
descendants of those
who settled
where the earth
is upside down

how far?
eleven thousand
risky miles
from my island to yours . . .
plus a few dark lines

those crooks and addicts
you counsel
the ones Jesus said
we would always
have with us

the young one
settled on the end
of my bed
sleeping off
some unwise excesses

let it sink in
sunlight or clear cold
voices and children
what matters
matters everywhere

~New Zealand / *England*

Tony Beyer is a New Zealander whose poetry has appeared in international journals and publications for several decades. 'what matters' is his first collaborative work.

Joy McCall is a nurse/counsellor, retired because of paraplegia following a motorcycle crash. She has written all kinds of poetry for 50 years, publishing occasionally here and there. She lives on the edge of the old walled city of Norwich, England, having spent much of her life in Canada. She treasures most her loved ones, nature, books, words and tattoos, life, and poetry. Keibooks published her 'circling smoke, scattered bones', 'hedgerows' and 'rising mist, fieldstones'. She thanks M. Kei for his constant support.

Vyonne McLelland-Howe

up the path
my old dog walks
struggling
on arthritic legs
we meet in the middle

new shoes
in my cupboard
with heels
much shorter now—
puppy play time

~*Australia*

Vyonne McLelland-Howe lives in Wollongong in New South Wales, on the eastern coast of Australia. She is retired and finds great pleasure in writing tanka. Her tanka have been published in Australian and international publications.

A Note about Ryuka

Ryoh Honda

Ryuka is another tanka. It literally means "song of Ryukyu," the old name of Okinawa, the islands located on the southwest edge of Japan. Although now Okinawa is one of the 47 prefectures in the country, as the Ryukyu Kingdom, it was an independent nation during 1429–1879. The Ryukyu Kingdom was culturally rich and performing arts played an important role in their social system, especially in their diplomatic purpose, for the kingdom had to take a delicate political balance between China and Japan.

Up to the present time, Okinawa boasts its own unique cultural assets. Their opera, *kumiodori*, for example, is on the UNESCO list of Intangible Cultural Heritage of Humanity. Also, Okinawa islands where sacred rites have been performed for several centuries, are full of important intangible folk culture properties. So the islands still preserve the traditional base of their own songs and poems. *Omoro-sousi*, the oldest anthology of local songs and poems, was compiled by the royal government during 1532 and 1623. The anthology is often called Okinawa's *Man'yoshu* (mainland Japan's premier anthology of classical poetry). After *omoro*, which have relatively flexible metric forms, ryuka emerged as a new style fixed form song in the 17th century, under the influence of mainland waka and the penetration of *sanshin*, a three stringed musical instrument. Since then, ryuka acquired popularity rapidly and broadly.

Among the several forms of ryuka, the most dominant form consists of 30 sound units, or 'on', in four phrases of 8-8-8 and 6 sound units respectively. Okinawa people call this basic ryuka form *san pachi roku* (three eight six), as it is made of 3 lines of 8 sound units followed by the last line of 6 sound units. Also, there are forms called *nakafu*, mixed style with waka. Their forms are 5-7-8-6 or sometimes 5-5-8-6 and 7-7-8-6.

The oldest ryuka anthology is *Ryuka-hyakkou*, compiled in the end of 18th century. It consists of three volumes, each mentions around two hundred ryuka, classified by roughly one hundred types of tunes. All other old ryuka anthologies contains both scores and words. This implies ryuka was basically composed to sing, while waka was generally made to intone or to be read. It should be noted that in classic ryuka, names of poets are known only for some; many of the old ones are anonymous,

For composing ryuka practically in English, the number of sound units in the local language should be adjusted so that the English version can fully leverage the original ryuka form, because English has more diversified and dynamic syllabic system than Okinawan language (*Uchinaaguchi*) and so the amount of meaning in a poem could be swollen significantly if the number of English syllables is applied to that of sound units of the local language. Accordingly, it would be comfortable if an accented syllable in English could be counted as two sound units in the original language of ryuka to keep not only length and underlying rhythm of the form but also the amount of sounds and meaning in the poem. This method is also applicable to waka and tanka. For, in a sense, there are no syllables in Okinawan language and also in Japanese. The etymology of "syllable" is Greek *syllabae*, meaning "gathering together." The vowels of Okinawan and Japanese, however, do not gather consonants around them as English does. Their vowels rather just attach one consonant before them, and no consonants followed after the vowels. Also, 'n' is regarded as an independent sound unit.

I believe we can enjoy universal ryuka and tanka in various ways. Adjusting the number of syllables in English to the sound units of two languages in the Far East would be one of the ways to do so.

Ryoh Honda is a kajin (tanka poet) in Tokyo, Japan. Enjoying tanka practice, he publishes his works, tanka reviews, and essays in some journals occasionally.

Liam Wilkinson's poetry has appeared in such journals as Modern English Tanka, Presence, Paper Wasp, Atlas Poetica, Simply Haiku, Bottle Rockets, Skylark, Lynx and many others. He has served as editor of Prune Juice, 3LIGHTS and Modern Haiga. He lives in North Yorkshire, England, and his website can be found at ldwilkinson.blogspot.co.uk

Weaponness: Climbing Towards an Understanding of Ryūka

Essay and Ryūka by Liam Wilkinson

I put on my one pair of shoes
My one too-small, too-tight jacket
And set out for old Weaponness
My hill away from home

From the summit of Weaponness
I gather all my belongings
On one side, a sprawling grey sea
On the other, field smells

Many years ago, I lived in the Weaponness Valley, a charming area of the British coastal resort of Scarborough. Weaponness is the old Roman name for the steep wooded hill that looms over Scarborough's South Bay. Today, this dark and imposing hill is referred to as Oliver's Mount, many believing that Oliver Cromwell once sited battalions there. But the surrounding district, with its deep, green valley and Victorian town houses which appear to tumble down the mount's slope is, even today, referred to as *Weaponness*—meaning, literally, *defensive point of land.*

From the summit of Weaponness, one is afforded a magnificent view of the Yorkshire coast, its black jagged edges sprawling to both the north and south. Cornelian and Cayton Bays, little paradises of largely ignored coves, can be seen to the south whilst the white spray of the ever unsettled sea to the north is interrupted by two notable structures—that of Scarborough's medieval Royal fortress, once home to Richard III and now in romantic ruins, and the Grand Hotel, which was famously mentioned in Arthur Rimbaud's *Illuminations.* Sailing a few miles further north would deliver you to the enchantingly named coastal settlements of Ravenscar and Robin Hood's Bay, before arriving at the tall ship-strewn harbour of Whitby, where Bram Stoker penned *Dracula* and Captain Cook became a seaman.

Twelve years have swiftly passed since I resided in one of those cold, shabby town houses that stand on the last shelf of Weaponness before the land gives way to the deep scar of the Valley Road. Twelve years since I would wake each morning and climb the path towards the summit of Weaponness, down along its dirt trails and to the edge of the cliff at Holbeck, where I would sit and write the poems of a young mind, beguiled by the surrounding multifarious landscape. And yet, I return here regularly—several times a month, in fact—to feed these views to my soul and soothe my mostly landlocked feet and work-addled mind with sea-soaked rocky ascents.

Steam of night lifts from the valley
These hills appear to be breathing
I too am alive this morning!
I declare from my sill

You are welcome, soft red dawn sun
To my tatty little hill hut
Where, all night, I've penned ryūka
Under a cold, dim moon

Whether or not I am *physically* able to wind my way up the sinuous paths of Weaponness, I frequently allow my mind to traverse that landscape, which has become such a necessary place of meditation and solitude, via the quatrains of ryūka—a short poetic form originating in the Ryukyu Islands of Japan; a cousin of tanka, which arrived in the kingdom, inspiring the native Ryukyuans after the Satsuma invasion of 1609. Having studied poetry at a college that, itself, sits on the edge of Weaponness, that rugged point of coastal land has always seemed, to me, a poetic place. It was there, many moons ago, that I discovered the haiku of Basho, the tanka of Saigyo and the mountain poems of Han Shan. It was there that I penned my first naïve attempts at haiku, senryu and tanka. It was also there that I heard the first echoes of Onna Nabe and Yoshiya Chiru, the most notable writers of ryūka.

I find in next-to-nothingness
Many charming, glistening gifts
Such silence spoils me rotten
Such stillness holds me tight

A day without its voice wakes up
I stand on my mountain, silent
Somewhere, on a nearaway beach
The swash beats a barrel

Like its tanka cousin, ryūka has musical roots. Its four lines, with a syllable pattern of 8-8-8-6, were originally composed to be sung. These short folk songs were accompanied by the *sanshin*, an Okinawan instrument with three strings, and carried in their lines the voices of average Ryukyuan people, engaged in their everyday activities.

Lost in these soft, delicate tastes
And the charming click of chopsticks
I am content to eat alone
Up here on Weaponness

Weaponness is home to many
Houses cling for life to its slopes
Sheep and cows graze on its wet grass
A poet drinks its views

I find a suitable spot on the slopes of Weaponness, where I may sit and rest my eyes on the sea's horizon line, before plunging into my notebook with a sharpened pencil. I think about Onna Nabe, that simple eighteenth century farm girl, trapped by the controlling politics and social conventions of the Ryukyu kingdom, climbing the Onna Mountain that loomed over her village with a yearning heart and infusing her ryūka with a determined voice that would, without these brief poems, be subdued by her time. There, in the music of ryūka, Onna Nabe found the freedom to express her radical views and protest against the restraints the government had cast upon her land.

There's a child in me who wishes
To, one day, roll down this steep hill
And come to a stop only when
He reaches the ocean

The sun leans against my bald head
Soft breezes sniff at my creased coat
I've woken from my midday nap
Half a mile from the ground

I think of poor Yoshiya Chiru, the seventeenth century child concubine who, unlike Onna Nabe, found herself completely imprisoned from birth but, with her literary prowess, discovered an outlet via ryūka. And when I think of her tragically short life—she committed suicide at the age of eighteen—and how much her poetry must have meant to her, I am glad to have found a friend in ryūka, away from the complexities of modern life, high up on my peak.

What shapes we human beings make
Such serpentine pathways we forge
In my mind, there is a straight road
That leads to Weaponness

Evening sun makes Weaponness smile
I leave it there, stilled in amber
For I must plunge towards my hut
Before night steals the paths

Today, the Ryukyu Islands are vastly different to those inhabited by Onna Nabe and Yoshiya Chiru, but ryūka is still written by natives and those who have moved away from the islands. It is even incorporated into traditional Ryukyuan dance and many a *sanshin* master coats his melodies with those brief folk songs. But the spirit of ryūka—that ache for freedom, for boundless love and life—is something which affects us all as we traverse the dark landscapes of our tempestuous world. For me, the winds of Weaponness and the brief breaths of ryūka are one and the same. The music of ryūka is as universal as that of tanka and haiku, of the humorous dodoitsu and the sharp-edged senryu, and the peak of Weaponness is my own Mount Onna. And whether we English-language writers are sticking strictly to the 8-8-8-6 syllable pattern, finding new paths through a looser long-long-long-short pattern or experimenting with freer expressions, we all have a little ryūka waiting within us.

The Explosion of Tanka

Patricia Prime

There's nothing new about tanka, although we now see it in various guises: one, two, three, four or five line tanka, to six line forms such as sedoka and cherita. There are also experimental akarui. Many groups now study and write tanka and the interest in the form now finds a place in social media that brings tanka to the fore with the use of email, Twitter, Facebook, blogs, online journals and YouTube.

Tanka ('short song') were an important part of Japanese court poetry even before the first written records were compiled. In Japanese, tanka were written in one or two lines made up of five phrases with a total of 31 sound units. The traditional pattern in English being short, long, short, long, long lines (5-7-5-7-7).

Recently I was asked to look at the tanka on YouTube written and performed by three well-known tanka poets: Genie Nakano, Peter Fiore and the symphonic poem "Five Levels Of The Watershed", at SoundBubble that features the tanka of M. Kei.

Where to begin? Perhaps with the obvious: that I was struck by these artists' performances, wit and liveliness. Their humour is already familiar to me from my reading of their work in various books, journals and online publications.

Let me make it clear from the outset that my critique is written from my perspective as a reader, writer and editor of tanka, and not as a viewer. I make no distinction between spoken word artists, performance poets, balladeers or poets who express themselves on CDs—all are poets, writing poetry.

The unwillingness of publishers to publish poetry books may have led to the rise of poets performing their work on various videos via YouTube. This venue provides poetry writers with the means to reproduce their tanka in spoken performances, in the same way that a musical score or dramatic script is reproduced. Like any other form, poetry undergoes change and reinvention. The present trend to express oneself via the social media sites contributes towards the proliferation of tanka.

Is there any other form of poetry more symbolic, more loaded with meaning, than the simple tanka? It encompasses, encapsulates and contains a field of human culture and social interaction. Surely it is no wonder individuals feel the urge to express themselves via the media. The symbolic value of presenting oneself to an audience—both in physical appearance and the actual content of the video, appeals to perhaps a handful of people writing tanka—but surely they may have an audience of hundreds, if not thousands, via YouTube, which make the benefits of performance worthy of discussion.

Genie Nakano is a poet, yoga and meditation instructor, dancer and performance artist. Nakano enjoys performing the spoken word with music and movement/dance at open mics and cultural events. In 'Orales Pues' she gives a recital of her tanka from her collection of tanka entitled *Storyteller*. Nakano is extremely expressive in her movements: she strokes her leg, runs her hand down her sides, over her breasts and stomach, waves her arms and moves around the stage, dancing and gesticulating. Here are two of her tanka from her performance entitled "Drone of the Dragon":

I watch
my hand's shadow as it moves
across the lines
it wants to write a poem
on this empty page

come dance with me
in the morning light
the wind is at our heels
let's leap . . .
above the gusts

Dance, with its forward, backward, sideways and circling motion, is something with which Nakano is clearly interested and her tanka are infused with the here and now, of existence as a state of flux.

Peter Fiore is well-known to readers of *Atlas Poetica* and the *Bright Stars* collections on Kindle.

He has been a writer for over 40 years and discovered gogyohka in 2008. In 2009, he published *text messages*, the first volume of American poetry totally devoted to gogyohka.

Here is a tanka from his performance:

our first time together
I last 2 minutes you get pregnant
fifty years later
we have 7 grandchildren
and live 5000 miles apart

Fiore moves over his subjects as well as into them. He is interested in what lies behind the words, the unknowable. And indeed it is as if he cannot get enough of the world and all its elements, as if he is breathing in all the stimuli around him. Inspiration in its true sense.

The SoundCloud composition, 'Five Levels Of The Watershed', played by the Chesapeake Bay Youth Symphony with live electronics can be found at the following site: <http://soundcloud.com/dubble8/five-levels-of-the-watershed-1>. There are five movements to the piece: 1. Ice Flows on the Upper Susquehanna, II. Chesepiooc (Native Names), III. Harborplace Soundscape, IV. Heron Sea and V. Submerged Islands. A detailed map of the Bay is also provided. Some excerpts from *Heron Sea* by M. Kei were provided to the students along with some harmonic structures. Spoken words by M. Kei can be heard in the *Heron Sea* section.

Kei accomplishes a difficult feat in 'Five Levels of The Watershed' as the sound is of an expansive range yet exacting form; one section of which includes his spoken voice. This is real-time music, in which the sound processes unfold in the same interval it takes to listen to them. The result is a collection 11.24 minutes of meticulously recorded sounds in which the scenery of the Bay serves to direct a quicksilver flow of associative thought. M. Kei calls our attention equally to the subtle cinematic shifts of "the musical tones of halyards", "the great blue heron", "watermen grown old", "wooden boats" and "men gone to their graves"; all the while tracking resolutely each momentary realisation sparked by sensory phencmena. 'Five Levels Of The Watershed' is a perceptive and connective piece, employing perfect blocks of sound which seem to have been grafted from the nebulous atmosphere of the Bay and segued intrinsically within the symphonic piece.

The tanka and their performances have the capacity to fuse the physical, the emotional, the lexical and the spoken voice in what is ultimately a celebration of the word. One of things I like best about the YouTube videos is the way in which they take pleasure in the words and personalities. The words become charged vehicles of life, not separate from the person but an extension of poet. In these videos, language becomes an extension of the body too. This is a site to savour, not just for its sensual delights but for its insight into the richness that lies below tanka's fascinating surfaces.

Substructure in Tanka: The Strophe, Line, and Poetic Phrase

by M. Kei

In discussing tanka, it is necessary to define what we mean by different terms, and that poses certain problems when discussing substructures within the form. 'Verse' is usually used to mean the whole stanza, or an individual line, so 'verse' is too confusing to use in tanka. Tanka have three levels of structure: the poetic phrase, what I call the 'strophe', and the poem itself. For our purposes, a strophe is one or more lines grouped together to form a substructure within the tanka. Strophes may be of different lengths, but they form a coherent unit of prosody and meaning.

Notice that 'sentence' and 'clause' are not structures in tanka; tanka may possess formal grammar or they may not. Sentences and clauses may make up a line, strophe, or the entire poem, or they may be subdivided in various ways.

Likewise the 'line,' although often referenced in tanka, is not exactly how Japanese tanka are structured. Tanka are made up of five parts which in Japanese are usually written on one line, but sometimes two or three, or wherever the calligrapher finds convenient to break the poem. Most Westerners are so accustomed to the line as a unit of poetry that many, maybe even most, tanka in English depend upon the line as a unit of organization. Skilled poets can create a complex interplay of Western and English structures to enrich their tanka. Thus 'line' is a useful concept for interpreting tanka written in English, but not in Japanese.

This raises the question of whether enjambment is a legitimate technique in tanka. It is, although it is often seen in poems whose author knows only that tanka consists of a certain number of syllables per line. Such simplistic understanding ignores the Japanese structure of five poetic parts that makes up tanka: A single run-on sentence can be perfectly formatted to fit the sanjuichi structure of 5-7-5-7-7 syllables, but that doesn't make it a tanka. The question is, how are the parts arranged? The rhythm and relationships created by the interaction of the five fundamental units is the defining feature of tanka. It is why tanka is a formal form and not simply five lines of free verse.

I shall use the term 'poetic phrase,' or just 'phrase,' to refer to one of these five fundamental units of tanka structure. A 'phrase' in tanka is the smallest unit of prosody and meaning. It may be a word, clause, fragment, sentence, or any combination thereof. A phrase might even be made of a punctuation mark (rare) or several sentences (also rare).

The question is, what are the substructures that make the tanka work? This is a difficult analysis for a reader not familiar with the conventions of tanka. It is also why tanka appear deceptively simple to the neophyte. Not until a person sits down to try and write them do they discover how difficult it is.

Western terminology often fails to capture the element under discussion, so a variety of Japanese terms have been adopted into English to discuss tanka. Where no good English equivalent is available, or where the connotations are distinctly different, I will use the Japanese. For example, the *mono no aware* is a *memento mori*, but the connotations are different. The former invokes a pleasurable sadness or appreciation of perishable beauty, the latter is an omen of impending death casting its shadow over the pleasures of the world. The Christian who believes in eternal damnation for his sins views death quite differently from the Buddhist who believes he will be reincarnated according to his merits.

To understand the various parts that make up a tanka, let us consider some examples.

I could tell
from the look in her eyes
the cancer had spread
from her lungs to her liver
and into both our lives

Barbara Robidoux, *Take Five : Best Contemporary Tanka*, Vol. 1. MET Press, 2009.

Here it is broken into strophes:

I could tell
from the look in her eyes

the cancer had spread
from her lungs to her liver

and into both our lives

In Robidoux's tanka, L1-2, L3-4, L5 are strophes. This follows the old tanka pattern dating back to the Man'yoshu, but also classical Greek plays. Notice the movement: from "I" the speaker, to "her" back to "us." Left, right, center. You could dance Robidoux's tanka. Move left on the first strophe, right on the second strophe, back to center on the third. In Greek plays, strophes were motions in time to verses; hence 'strophe' refers both to verses and to movements.

Robidoux's tanka is composed of one complete sentence (minus punctuation marks).

The reader unfamiliar with tanka conventions might read this simply as a sentence and miss the substructures at work. Notice that L2 and L4 both begin with the word "from". Each of the first two strophes has a parallel structure: a statement that could be a complete sentence on its own (I could tell, the cancer had spread), but followed by a clause that expands it. Each of the clauses contains a reference to "her" and her body parts: her eyes, her lungs, her liver. The third strophe is much shorter and the changed rhythm creates a sense of finality that closes the poem so that we know it's done, but it also creates a sense of doom so that we know that the outcome of the cancer is fatal. The unnamed "her" is dying. Structure is perfectly matched to meaning with the two amplifying each other.

The first strophe begins the action with the self, the "I" that observes, then moves away to the Other that is the subject of the poem, then returns to center with "us." This distinguishes the poem from tanka that are merely observations by starting from a place of apparent separation, only to draw the speaker into the subject's doom. Many novice tanka writers write observations and format them as verses; the use of the authorial "I" is like the photographer's shadow falling into the image. It distances us from the subject. Robidoux's tanka subverts that expectation by dragging the "I" into the action. The "I" of the poem is a passive observer, but as the final line moves into "both our lives," the power of the subject pulls the passive and helpless "I" into it. The inability of "I" to take action or to resist what is happening further enhances the sense of doom. There is nothing that can be done. The poem is over, the death is final. The "I" is incapable of doing anything more than sounding the anguish.

The strophe is not the same as a 'jo,' which I discussed in a previous article.[1] However, a strophe may contain a jo, literally 'preface,' a commonly employed technique in tanka dating back to the earliest tanka of the Man'yoshu. The jo usually came at the beginning as its name indicates, but already in the Man'yoshu era poets

---

[1] 'Tanka Structure: The 'Jo' or 'Preface''. *Atlas Poetica* 13. Autumn, 2012.

experimented with putting it in different places. The original jo was commonly a two-line strophe (L1–2), with the body of the poem being placed on L3–5. This is related to the choka in which an unlimited number of couplets could precede the three-line ending.

First, a tanka with a conventional jo forming the first strophe:

> hot august
> an open fire hydrant
> flushes out
> the whole under-ten
> neighbourhood

Art Stein, *Take Five : Best Contemporary Tanka*, Vol. 1. MET Press, 2009.

> hot august
>
> an open fire hydrant
> flushes out
> the whole under-ten
> neighbourhood

L1, "hot august," is a conventional jo—it gives some basic information. In Japanese tanka, the jo frequently contained a conventional epithet about a place or other subject. We see the same here; "hot august" is a conventional statement that is not original to the author, but it provides useful information that sets the scene for the strophe to come. If the jo is omitted, the remaining body still forms a coherent unit of prosody and meaning. In order to be a jo, it must be fungible; that which cannot be changed without changing the meaning of the poem is the body.

L2–5 is a single strophe. It contains two substructures within it (L2–3 and L4–5). The substructures are units of prosody and meaning, but not coherent on their own. They require each other to create a complete strophe. Each of these substructures is composed of two phrases. The component parts are set up in parallel to one another. The four line body is one strophe made up of two substructures, each of which is made up of two phrases forming a coherent whole,

introduced by a classical jo.

Next, a poem in which the first two lines appear to be a jo, but are not:

> our white cat
> gone seven years
> and still
> her light
> in every room

Alexis Rotella, *Take Five : Best Contemporary Tanka*, Vol. 1. MET Press, 2009.

> our white cat
> gone seven years
>
> and still
>
> her light
> in every room

L1–2 are the body of the poem. Without L1–2, the rest of the poem makes no sense. Since L1–2 are essential to comprehending the poem, they are not a jo. (Compare with Art Stein's tanka above.) This is also a reminder that while a jo often contains an image, not all images are jo.

L1 creates a clear image of a white cat that fades into a ghostly presence when we learn it is "gone seven years." The image is clear, but the emotional content is not yet revealed. We don't know if this will be an amusing anecdote, a threnody over the loss of a beloved pet, or something else. This is especially the case with a poet as diverse as Alexis Rotella. She writes humorous kyoka on the subject of death as well as human foibles, so there's no knowing what is coming until it's read.

L3 "and still" is composed of two words that do not usually merit being placed on a line by themselves, but in this case, they perform the valuable function of subdividing the poem into three strophes while prolonging the suspense and heightening anticipation. The fulcrum on which the first and third strophes balance is L3; its neutrality slips from our awareness and leaves the first and third strophes in perfect balance.

The jo can be used to subdivide a tanka into a wide variety of patterns. The courtiers of the Man'yoshu era started this experimentation, and anglophone poets have continued to diversify the jo. By understanding what a jo is, we are better able to recognize the strophes that make up a tanka. However, that means we must also be prepared for unusual uses of the jo and complex structures.

The next tanka divides the jo itself:

it glides towards me
as I sit at the harbor
in our time apart
trying not to think of you—
the sailboat without a sail

Thelma Mariano, *Fire Pearls : Short Masterpieces of the Human Heart.* Keibooks, 2006.

it glides towards me

as I sit at the harbor
in our time apart
trying not to think of you—

the sailboat without a sail

In this case, L1 and L5 form the jo and are a single strophe that has been split by placing the body squarely in the middle. Splitting the jo into two parts echoes the narrator's separation from "you." A lesser poet would have kept "it glides towards me" and "the sailboat without a sail" together. Formatting the sailboat so that it approaches the narrator, then disappears from the body of the poem, only to reappear at the end without a sail, replicates the circumstances of the narrator's relationship. Splitting a jo was not done in the old Japanese poems, but in Mariano's hands is highly effective.

Next we have a poem with three jo and four strophes:

cold wind
divorce papers served
the bottom falling out
of a distant cloud
rainshower

susan delphine delaney, *Fire Pearls : Short Masterpieces of the Human Heart.* Keibooks, 2006.

cold wind

divorce papers served

the bottom falling out
of a distant cloud

rainshower

L1's "cold wind" is a conventional jo that introduces "divorce papers served." The image sets the mood for the body. The body, however, is very brief. It occupies L2 only. L3–4 are a second jo that provide an extension of the first jo, and L5 is yet another jo, piling up yet another weather image. The stacking of multiple jo is like a stack of bricks falling on the narrator's head. Each chilly wet weather image intensifies the misery of the poem while providing clues as to the probable sequence of events. The strength of the body is such that it is able to support the unusual asymmetric trio of jo.

Unlike in the previous poem, each jo is an independent strophe, not the divided parts of a single strophe. The fragmenting of the poem into multiple small, but meaningful, units echoes the emotional fragmentation of the narrator.

As we have seen, the jo is a common and valuable technique in tanka, but tanka can be written very well without it.

her skirt brightens
in the sunlight at the door—
quick! quick!
her scissor shadow
cuts me through

Larry Kimmel, *Fire Pearls : Short Masterpieces of the Human Heart.* Keibooks, 2006.

her skirt brightens
in the sunlight at the door—

quick! quick!

her scissor shadow
cuts me through

Kimmel's tanka is composed of three strophes: L1–2, L3, and L4–5. Omitting L3, we have a sequence of actions in which a woman's skirt appears in the doorway and the shadow of her legs limned by the sun evokes a strong reaction in the narrator. As strong as the action is, it isn't complete without L3. The double imperative divides the first and third strophes from each other, and sets up a swift rhythm like a pair of scissors swiftly snipping or a racing heart. It is L3 that gives the poem its sense of movement as well as enhancing the reaction to the experience.

L3 is a pair of sentences. Each imperative sentence is only one word long, and the lack of capitals de-emphasizes the importance of the sentence as a structure, but they're still sentences. The poet has omitted capitals and most punctuation within the poem to subvert English grammar; thus we read the two sentences of L3 as a single strophe, not as a pair of short strophes. Consider the poem with correct capitalization and punctuation. The poem loses energy and subtlety:

Her skirt brightens
in the sunlight at the door—
Quick! Quick!
Her scissor shadow
cuts me through.

The doubled action of L3 is essential to keep the poem moving and to unify its various parts. Grammatically correct capitalization would have put too much weight on it, slowing down the movement and dulling the sensation of a racing heart. "Quick!" would not suffice; the double "quick! quick!" sets up three parallel pairs: two legs, two blades of scissors, two exclamations. It also puts each strophe into parallel form: all three strophes are made up of two parts of equal weight. Nonetheless, the de-emphasis of English grammar lets us read L3 as a single strophe, rather then emphasizing the pair of parts. Our ear hears the music even if we don't consciously register why.

Larry Kimmel is a master of complex structures within tanka. He is equally adroit at exploiting both Japanese and Western units of construction.

this past August,
all at once, the abuse of a decade
condensed into a bullet—
    there's a house for sale
    in our neighborhood

Larry Kimmel, *Take Five : Best Contemporary Tanka*, Vol. 1. MET Press, 2009.

this past August,

all at once, the abuse of a decade
condensed into a bullet—

    there's a house for sale
    in our neighborhood

L1 is a conventional jo that sets the scene and raises the temperature for what is to come. L2–5 is a sequence of events that forms the body of the poem. That body is divided into two strophes. Each strophe is strong enough to stand on its own, but they require each other to complete the tanka. Each of these strophes is built of different parts. L2–3 is composed of the clause "all at once" that belongs to the sentence "the abuse of a decade condensed into a bullet". Each strophe is a coherent unit of meaning.

Reading tanka successfully means being able to follow the Japanese system of structure as opposed to the Western. This is one of many reasons why a tanka is not simply a five line free verse. It is also why so many tanka poets omit standard punctuation and capitals; they have intuitively grasped that including standard English grammar would obscure the Japanese system at work. Only a handful of tanka poets, such as Alexis Rotella and Denis Garrison, use conventional punctuation and capitalization, and they do so deliberately as they harness English grammar in support of their structures.

The second strophe opens with "all at once" and closes with an emdash—two markers setting off the action of the sentence with indicators of speed. The enjambment at the end of L2 imposes a small hesitation as the trigger is squeezed, then the bullet is fired on L3. The opening and closing of this strophe resembles the lines graphic artists use to generate the sensation of speed.

The third strophe on L4–5 is indented to abruptly transition to a different topic, a topic that by its juxtaposition is clearly related to and the result of the action in the second strophe. Very often poets with less skill than Kimmel use indentations and other spacings to create a sense of structure where one is lacking. In Kimmel's tanka, it is the innate rhythm and structure of the poem that creates the format, not the other way around.

Poets who are developing their craft should focus on building structure into their words so they will not be at the mercy of the typesetter. It has happened more than once that a typesetter unfamiliar with tanka has set them all flush left, sometimes even on four lines! If the poem loses its structure and cohesion due to a typesetter's error, then it was weak to begin with. Kimmel's poem does not lose anything by being set flush left; the structure is inherent to the poem.

> this past August,
> all at once, the abuse of a decade
> condensed into a bullet—
> there's a house for sale
> in our neighborhood

Even more complex structures can be created by varying line length and placement. The use of hypometric and hypermetric lines is acceptable in anglophone tanka and is a reflection of the fact that the English syllable is not the same as the Japanese sound unit. For example, the English word "stretched" is only one English syllable, but seven Japanese sound units: s-t-re-t-ch-e-d. If we count it as one syllable, we wind up with a line far longer than the Japanese. Furthermore, Japanese sound units are much less variable in length and form than English syllables. For example, "radio

diva" is five syllables, but consumes about the same amount of time to say and space to write as "stretched." Some critics have gone as far as suggesting English writers stick to one and two syllables words. While simplicity in language is a desirable feature, the right word is the word that works, regardless of length.

> Against the door dead leaves are falling;
> On your window the cobwebs are black.
> Today, I linger alone.
>
> The foot-step?
> A passer-by.

Jun Fujita, *Tanka: Poems in Exile*. Chicago: Covici-McGee Co., 1923.

Fujita's tanka contains three strophes with two jo, L1-2 and L4-5. The body of the poem is a short L3. The inclusion of a personal pronoun on L2 blurs, but does not erase, the distinction between the first jo and the body. Deciding how to interpret the structures in this complex tanka is fraught with problems. The hypermetric length of L1 and L2 suggests interpreting them as single units in themselves, but the two are clearly related to one another and make a complete scene. It is apparent that the door and the window belong to the same house. The use of the semi-colon tells us that we are to read the two lines together as a single strophe even if they grammatically form two sentences.

We have already learned not to suffer the tyranny of English grammar, but the scrupulous use of punctuation and capitalization in this poem requires us to examine it. When we do so, we note careful structures set up to create units of prosody and meaning. English grammar cannot be discarded in interpreting this tanka, even though it was written by a Japanese American poet.

L3 is the body of the poem. Although it fits with L4–5 as a coherent series of actions, the blank line separating the two shows that the poet did not intend us to read them that way. If the gap were closed, the poet's intended structure would not be as clear, which is a flaw, but it is a small one, since the intended structure is still discernible.

Divided into its strophes, it is:

Against the door dead leaves are falling;
On your window the cobwebs are black.

Today, I linger alone.

The foot-step?
A passer-by.

The hypermetric first strophe serves to extend the subjective experience of the narrator's waiting. The reader knows the narrator has been waiting a very long time just from this. Then, the two short lines of the third strophe simulate the quickening of the poet's pulse when he hears someone approaching. Anticipation swiftly turns to disappointment as the passer-by is no one that interests the narrator.

In between, L3, the body of the poem, reports the narrator's problem, "I linger alone." The use of the word "today" makes it clear that he was not always alone. It also indicates that in spite of how long he's been waiting, he hopes that it will soon be over. Thus the use of the word "today" implies that this is not the first time he's been disappointed, just as it is not the first day he's been waiting.

The five poetic phrases that make up the poem are clear. In spite of the highly variable line length, irregular 'upside down' structure, and conventional English grammar, each line is a unit of prosody and meaning. In other words, each line is a 'phrase,' in the tanka meaning of the word. The varying length of the lines serves the meaning and rhythm.

As mentioned previously, enjambment is a legitimate technique for tanka, although it is most frequently encountered in the work of novice poets who are counting syllables. Sometimes, however, the tanka form is adopted by skilled poets from other traditions who make something very different of it. This is most noticeable in the work of African American tanka poets going back to the Harlem Renaissance. Today, the Black poet who has had the greatest influence on

Black tanka poets is Sonia Sanchez.

Sanchez's work is heavily enjambed to make her thirty-one syllables fit the sanjuichi form. Unlike amateur poets, Sanchez has a superb command of image and line. Her line breaks are not forced to fit the pattern, instead the pattern is melded with her language.

i kneel down like a
collector of jewels before
you. i am singing
one long necklace of love my
mouth a sapphire of grapes.

Sonia Sanchez, *Shake Loose My Skin: New and Selected Poems*. Beacon Press, 1999.

If we reformat Sanchez's work, we can see that she has intuitively grasped the five part structure of tanka:

i kneel down like
a collector of jewels before you
i am singing
one long necklace of love
my mouth a sapphire of grapes

The lyricism and richly sensual imagery are very suitable for tanka. Tanka as a genre has a long history of love poetry, and Sanchez's work fits very well in that tradition. Her imagery is striking, erotic, and powerful.

But Sanchez didn't give us a tanka in which the lines correspond to the poetic phrases. She enjambed her work. With a poet of Sanchez's stature, we can be certain that she did it on purpose.

i kneel down like a
collector of jewels before
you.

i am singing
one long necklace of love my
mouth a sapphire of grapes.

Sanchez's poem divides into two nearly equal strophes with the break coming on L3 after the word "you." The line breaks placed after the word "a" at the end of L1 and "before" on L2 create a hesitation that strengthens the usual pause for line breaks. This in turn puts greater emphasis on the first word of the following lines, "collector" and "you."

Whatever image was evoked in the reader's mind by "kneel down," it was probably not "collector of jewels." Her unusual choice of image surprises us, and she will keep surprising us with her line breaks and word choices. (What is a "sapphire of grapes?") The emphasis given to "collector" and "you" enhances the erotic appeal.

Now that we have been introduced to the "collector of jewels," we can't help imagining an act of oral sex with the poet kneeling before a man. The position is often seen as submissive, even degraded, but the poet puts herself in the active role as a "collector of jewels." The "you" is not capitalized, reducing its importance even though its position first on L3 emphasizes its importance. In this tanka, a powerful woman is sexually in charge, even when she takes a position conventionally interpreted as submissive.

The mood is worshipful as she sings in the second strophe. Again the unusual imagery, "a necklace of love" and a "sapphire of grapes" startle with their vividness and provide a graceful depiction of something usually interpreted as crude or lewd. Specifically, the act of a male ejaculating on a woman's breasts is often called a "pearl necklace." The "necklace" and the narrator's kneeling position suggest that reading, but the "sapphire of grapes" subverts it. Once again the line break after "my" creates a hesitation that warns us L5 is not going to be what we expect. Furthermore, the placement of "my" at the end of L4 draws attention to it and reinforces the narrator's control over both the male subject and the reader's expectations.

Opening L5 with "mouth" draws us back to "singing." The narrator is singing her song to her lover, and the poet is singing her poem to the reader. "Mouth" supports an erotic interpretation, especially given the previous images. It is a teasing, powerful, love song by a woman in full command of herself both sexually and as a poet. That she depicts her mouth as a

jewel is a sign of her confidence, but why sapphire? The usual metaphors for a mouth depend on the colors red and pink. Blue is probably not even a reference to lipstick, although lipstick these days can be of any color. "Sapphire" and "grapes" together suggest a bluish purple that might be intended to represent the skin color of an African American, in this case, flushed with lust. If so, then "sapphire" is a symbol for lips. Grapes, with their plump, juicy shape and their long association with eroticism, further this interpretation.

This beautiful and complicated poem presents us with another choice: Do we try to analyze it in order to make sense of it? Or do we let it be and let the sounds and images wash over us and take us into a blissful revery of erotic possibilities? If we are simply readers, then the latter if sufficient. Enjoy the poem for its own sake. But if we are thoughtful critics who want to understand why the poem works, we must let its structure guide us to understand what it is. When analyzing amateur poets we can never be sure we are finding what the poet intended, but when analyzing the work of one of the notable American poets of our time, we must assume every choice is a purposeful one.

Sanchez has been cited by Matsukaze and other African American poets as a powerful influence on their work. We can see it in the tanka below.

> grasp him by the ears
> listen to the rust-colored
> song sailing through his
> apricot veins . . . he must be
> the one to capture my soul

Orestes (now writing as Matsukaze), *Fire Pearls : Short Masterpieces of the Human Heart.* Keibooks, 2006.

The enjambment and striking imagery follow in Sanchez's footsteps, yet the imitation is imperfect. Although "song" is an unexpected word to follow "rust-colored", the hesitation induced by the line break does not strengthen the word "song." That in turn means the break after "his" on L3 is not as strong as it would have been if "song" had been placed at the end of L2.

"Song" distracts from the line break after "his." Matsukaze has mimicked Sanchez's break after "my" with a similar intent; it enhances the importance of the "he" who is the subject of the poem. Yet Sanchez nowhere stated the subject of her song; it is the reader's interpretation that makes it what it is. Matsukaze, however, makes it clear to us that he is singing to a beloved man. His poem is much easier to understand and depends upon the originality of description for its literary value.

grasp him by the ears
listen to the rust-colored
song sailing through his
apricot veins . . .

he must be
the one to capture my soul

When we break the tanka into its two substructures, we discover two simple strophes. The adroit manipulation of pause and anticipation we seen in Sanchez's work is absent here. What we have is a jejune work from a promising amateur. (This poem was written nine or ten years ago and is an early work from Matsukaze.) The vivid imagery and the unabashed eroticism set him aside from run-of-the-mill amateurs.

As important as it is to study and even imitate admired poets during the learning process, eventually the poet must master his medium. We see that growth in Matsukaze's later work:

in midsummer heat i cannot remain at home quiet and cloistered your betrayal loud

Matsukaze, *Bright Stars* 7. Keibooks, 2014.

Matsukaze's recent work is well informed by extensive study. He is particularly interested in alternate lineation in tanka. The one line tanka above with a complete lack of capitals and punctuation offers us a challenge: can we find the five parts that make up tanka?

in midsummer heat
i cannot remain
at home
quiet and cloistered
your betrayal loud

The five poetic phrases that make up the tanka are obvious. The structures within this tanka are a good deal more complex than his early work.

in midsummer heat

i cannot remain
at home
quiet and cloistered

your betrayal loud

When the poem is divided into its three strophes, its structure is clear. "In midsummer heat" is a one line jo with the body divided into two strophes spread over L2–5. "Quiet and cloistered" belongs with the middle strophe because L2–4 form a unit of prosody and meaning. The implied commas before and after the phrase may seem to indicate that it should be a strophe of its own, but it contains insufficient information to qualify as a 'unit of meaning' by itself. It is only when grouped with L2–3 that it makes sense.

This is a neatly balanced poem with L1 and L5 being of equal length, but not of equal power. The jo, "midsummer heat," is purely conventional, but it serves to set the tone for what follows. The middle strophe builds the sense of suffocating heat and pressure which is released in the third strophe. Although the narrator doesn't tell us what betrayal sounds like, the midsummer heat suggests that it must sound like thunder. Usually we prefer a more specific word to give the reader a clearer image, but in this case, the context suggests an appropriate sound without the poet needing to spell it out. The ability of the poet to command the unwritten word is an essential part of what makes a small poem like tanka effective.

Earlier I mentioned that poets should not be afraid of polysyllabic words—the right word is the right word. Here "cloistered" invokes the nun-like virtue of a monogamous wife. This in turn tells us that although the author is male, the narrator is female. The ease with which Matsukaze crosses the gender line is a hallmark of his style, and was present even in his early work.

Returning to the original monotanka, the single line without punctuation creates a sensation of seething anger as words are spit out between clenched teeth. Reading it like this, the voice naturally rises and becomes louder, becoming loudest at the end of the line, aptly on the word "loud." Prosody and meaning unite and reinforce one another.

This tanka has excellent bones. No matter how it winds up being formatted, it retains its structure. The authorial intent is maintained, no matter what a typesetter does to it.

In the beginning I defined a strophe as one or more lines grouped together to form a substructure within the tanka, but here we must acknowledge that there is no obligation for a strophe to coincide with line breaks. Phrases and strophes, like sentences and grammatical clauses, may all be enjambed in the hands of a skilled poet. The competing systems of Western line and Japanese phrase can be deliberately played off against each other in complex but meaningful ways. We have also seen that tanka can contain substructures that as of yet don't have a name. When we build up phrases or subdivide strophes, we discover parts of structure that are clearly intentional and effective, but discussing these intermediate structures is outside the scope of this article.

Understanding poetic phrases, how they combine to form strophes, and how we interpret certain common elements that appear in tanka, such as the jo, enable us to parse the author's intention. This in turn enhances our appreciation for their artistry. Tanka are far from the simple free verses they appear at first glance; the use of a Japanese system of structure, the subversion of English grammar, and the interplay of Western and Japanese concepts create small poems of great complexity and power.

M. Kei is a tall ship sailor and award-winning poet who lives on Maryland's Eastern shore. He is the editor of Atlas Poetica : A

Journal of World Tanka. He was the editor-in-chief of Take Five : Best Contemporary Tanka, Vols. 1–4, and the editor of Bright Stars, An Organic Tanka Anthology. His most recent collection of poetry is January, A Tanka Diary (2013). He is also the author of the award-winning gay Age of Sail adventure novels, Pirates of the Narrow Seas (blogspot.narrowseas.com). He can be followed on Twitter @kujakupoet, or visit AtlasPoetica.org.

Review: *Journeys: Getting Lost* by Carole Johnston

Reviewed by Patricia Prime

Journeys: Getting Lost
Carole Johnston
Georgetown, Kentucky, USA
Finishing Line Press, 2015
RRP: $US12.49
Pb. 30 pp.
Front cover by Hunter Armstrong and back cover by Rowan Johnston

Carole Johnston is a well-known contributor to both *Atlas Poetica* and the *Bright Stars* volumes of tanka which M. Kei initiated. Due to her extensive experience as a published tanka poet, her focus is on quality. *Journeys: Getting Lost* is her first published book and she is a poet to watch out for. It's not so much a collection as one breath-taking sequence of haiku, tanka and short poems that captures the emotions and honesty of a traveller. Johnston is a lone traveller, accompanied only by her camera.

The book takes the form of a journey, much as we see in Basho's writings. The sections are called 'Lost In The West,' 'Lost In Bluegrass' and 'Lost in Appalachia'. Johnston is a typical follower of Basho's adventures and one who tends to be practical, stoic, verbally articulate and sophisticated; the typical tourist is practically inept and undone by suburban living, but Johnston's tools are sharp, her eye is clear, and her ear is accurate. Her observations are her own, economically and often delightfully expressed. She has a flow of pithy imagery, whether it be

time traveler
on the road with Basho
watching stars spin
fireflies disappearing
I fill my brush with ink

or

silent drive
up the rain mountain
journey ends
alone with my mind
the seeker inside

The compression and containment necessitated by the haiku and tanka forms brilliantly matches the geography of her travels. The result is spare, elegant writing, such that will pass the test of time. You will never be far away from the West, the Bluegrass or Appalachia, but you can absolutely rely on a smooth enjoyable read.

The tanka are fresh and original and draw us in with their humour and technique. Indeed, Johnston manipulates the tanka so that one forgets syllable count, line length and other approaches. One is drawn to the honesty and immediacy of her observations, presented in the traditional juxtaposition of human and natural elements. Or just as effectively in the modern form of self-analysis that exudes the classical Japanese qualities, such as we see in the following tanka:

breath of pine
hitching the open road
vagabond
chanting the words
of poets before me

Like many tanka poets, Johnston addresses the everyday concerns of the traveller: heat, dust, rain, or seeing dead animals on the road:

deer carcass
on bluegrass backroad
cows feasting
I drive by

And yet, although she is keenly aware of the transience of life, Johnston cares for it and feels an empathy for the animals and plants within it. She also voices deeper ideas, and many of her tanka have a philosophical tone:

two days alone
driving the desert
road on the map
thin grey line to nowhere
I'm fasting on dust

These are powerful tanka expressed with candour and a direct appeal, as well as a certain simplicity, as in the following tanka:

hero's journey
seeking inside myself
I find a trickster
searching the whole
green world

Johnston remains both engaged and at the same time objective: passionate and yet an observer, as in

I charge
down the highway
crashing
into butterflies
rushing towards birth

Like Basho, Johnston celebrates nature and the natural life, but her poems touch the whole range of her experience as a lone traveller: joy and sadness, pleasure and pain, loneliness and discovery. The book reflects the full spectrum of Johnston's poetic vision, including haiku, tanka and short lyrical poems. Johnston's journey and spirit will speak to lovers of poetry and travel. The selection of poems presented here reflect the range and depth of her vision and their focus on the natural environment.

Review: *Dancing With Another Me* by Gerry Jacobson

Reviewed by Patricia Prime

Dancing With Another Me
Gerry Jacobson
Canberra, Australia, 2015
iGen4 Press
Pb. 24 pp.
ISBN: 978-0-9943002-0-1.
For purchase details please contact jacobson@netspeed.com.au

I enjoyed reading this book which begins with a simple and straightforward introduction by the author, Gerry Jacobson, in which he states that the inspiration for this book about dance was "empowered by June Staunton's 'somatic dance work'" and also says that he has "been a student for about fifteen years".

The book contains 23 tightly woven tanka prose of beautifully composed poems which enable the reader to play with the words and music of the poems, and to imagine the progression of the poet as he moves in the first poem "bypass" from "Waking slowly" after bypass surgery to the "journey is all" in the final poem.

This refreshing book proves that there is something in dance movements that not only enhances the body but captures the infinity of moments made precious by the response to music and movement. We see in "It doesn't matter" the laziness of the body as it begins to warm up: "muscles forgotten for three weeks" and in the concluding tanka Jacobson writes of the blissfulness of being able to dance again:

the dance pulsates
and my scarred heart
opens
closes . . . opens
tears in my eyes

It seems to me that the question one has to ask about the performance of a group of dancers is—what is it that one enjoys in the close proximity of another person who may be a stranger? The answer comes in "The transition," where the poet first becomes intimate with himself, but by the third time of contact there is "A sense of two cocoons. One around me. One around us both."

The poems draw us in, maybe appeal to each of our senses by turn, by getting us to adopt a different angle on dance; perhaps, a kind of dramatic harmony that has a way of getting us to identify with the poet, joining in his love of dance, hearing the music, feeling its beat in his words, as in "The observer," where he is able to let go of the movement and allow the dance to take over, as indicated in this lovely tanka:

letting go
of conscious movement
allowing
the dance to take over
the child to play

Each of the tanka prose poems pulls us straight into the situation in which Jacobson finds himself, as we see in "For these few minutes": "How easily my tears flow today. Moving with the ball. Stripped to the essence." After so much absorption into Jacobson's world of dance, we come to the point of trust. In "Pelvis rocks," for example, he senses the other dancers; his body becomes the choreographer. With years of working together, the dancers trust and respect each other.

"Boundaries" takes place at the start of the day:

it's 5.30
kookaburra cackles
our long dark night
is coming to an end
our dancing day approaches

In this poem, Jacobson and the other dancers have an all-day movement workshop.

He is apprehensive about working with an unknown partner, a man, and doesn't know how close he can come without overstepping the boundary. Two qualities in the following poem, "Inside sunbeam," make an immediate impression: the music—"Soul music. Cello. Kletzmer?"—and the closeness of family. "Wayfarer" takes place on a winter evening with "Dances of healing and reconciliation." This is not nostalgia, but is where the author has found peace and tranquillity in the dance.

Also striking is the formality of the structure of the title poem, "Dancing with another me." The form here—alternating prose and understated tanka—provides an assisted journey for the reader through the author's exploration of the connection of hands to heart and the power of contact work. This theme is continued in the next poem, "The comfort of hands," where "interlocking hearts" form a circle for a dance of peace. But just to be still is also important as seen in "Stillness moves":

in the dance
my arm moves so slowly
through space
towards stillness
but the stillness moves

There are further interactions in "Beyond words," the external and the internal: "Winter bites" and the class dwindles due to flu, but the poet's eyes fill with tears as he is "Stunned by the dancers." What the narrator does is shown to us in the prose and tanka of "Moving together" and what is suggested by the actions of the dancers, is reassuring the poet and he feels that "the dance / will go on forever."

In the dance class, the dancers are encouraged, when the dance is over, to draw, as witnessed in "Cool colours," where the poet says, "I'll travel the darkness / of my interior." A god-like feeling is invoked in the poet in "Some sort of god" as he demonstrates a movement of the dance. The people the narrator meets in the dance studio seem more than mere mortals. As we read through the poems, they seem to adopt a mythical role, as guardians of the dance, of contact with others, co-operating and relating to each other, as in this fine tanka from "On the edge":

tied down
joined at the hip
constrained . . .
yet all seems possible
in our dance together

"Until the music stops" depicts the dancers moving together, moving apart, but still feeling the connection with each other. The perfect tanka completes the picture:

dancing
those unshed tears
all that matters
is to be here
in the dance—together

In "Pas de deux" (a tanka sequence) there is a thread of longing and love. The brilliant blossoming of the dance as the couple move from "back to back" to "wanting the dance / to go on for ever," deserves mention. "Pas de trois" provides a contrast as the poet is "drawn in to this delicious trio" and says he wants "the trio more than my own dance."

Each tanka prose is a miniature drama: sometimes an exercise in intimacy, as in "My heart held," where dance is expressed as "a metaphor for life":

My dance feels restricted and rather linear. the *pas de deux* becomes contact work and spinal awareness. Later we realise that on another level it's an exercise in intimacy. Dance is a metaphor for life. How lucky we are to have this teaching.

"Ending" has a powerful and searing image as the dancers perform and the poet says: "I'm sad, very sad, that it's ending." The final tanka prose is "Leaf litter," which was published in *Atlas Poetica*, 2015, I quote it in its entirety:

I am the one who lies down in strange places. The wooden floor of a dance hall. The grass beside a road. Leaf litter on the forest floor. And I sleep instantly. The sleep of the tired dancer. The exhausted pilgrim.

Barefoot. Boots beside me. Or, beneath my head. More frequently now. Face down. Embracing the earth. The journey is slow. The journey is all.

> midwinter . . .
> a cold wooden floor
> dancer
> wrapped in a blanket . . .
> that dark inner core

Gerry Jacobson is a consummate student of the dance. His deeply felt tanka prose embodies a passion for what makes his life worthwhile. Empathy for his fellow dancers permeates the poems as does his intuitive feeling for music and movement. One has a sense of wonder and enjoyment in reading his lovely work.

Review: *This Tanka Whirl* by Sanford Goldstein

Reviewed by Patricia Prime

This Tanka Whirl
Sanford Goldstein
Colrain, Massachusetts
Winifred Press Books
2nd Ed. 2015
Pb. 49 pp.
ISBN-13: 978-0-9832298-9-6.
For details, please contact htpp://
larrykimmel.tripod.com

Originally published in 2001 by Clinging Vine Press, the republication of *This Tanka Whirl* by Sanford Goldstein has been reissued by Winifred Press. Four graphics and the etching, "Two small trees by a stream in moonlight," are by Kazuaki Wakui. The contents are divided into nine sections with some after-thoughts by Goldstein.

Goldstein has been writing and translating tanka for more than four decades. He is a recognised master of the form and is still writing at the age of 89. There can be no doubt that he is a fine tanka poet with a deserved international reputation. A binding theme of the collection is the biography of the man himself through the powerful dynamics of his personality, his late wife, teaching literature and writing.

This Tanka Whirl offers lyrical and emotive tanka. In poem after poem, the language in the book combines allusion, sensation and language, to reclaim a personal, collective and literary career. The book widens Goldstein's engagement with the past in "somersault tanka." This fine tanka is about the way in which he is haunted by the past:

> at times, mother,
> with your peripheral vision
> you called me by some other name
> as if you wanted
> twice the love

Goldstein's own construction and deconstruction of his long life is undertaken with words and imagery that seek to encapsulate the trials and pleasures of his life. Often he writes about his time as a Professor of English, teaching not only in the United States but in Japan, where he has lived for many years. His interest in literature focuses here on *Moby Dick* and *Hamlet:* the anguish of the protagonists mirroring Goldstein's own preponderance to dwell on the past and to think about the future—what might have been, what does the future hold? In a poem from "Moby Dick Tanka," he writes

> lift me,
> muse,
> into Ahab's language,
> dark peripheries
> surrounded by white

Goldstein's world is always existent and existential, and yet always, as he writes in the following tanka from "battering silence," his children give him great comfort:

the gorgeous
generosity
of my kid
tiptoeing along the edge
of tonight's roughness

In "body language," the focus is on Goldstein himself: he nods at his fellow lecturers in the corridor, is forced into the street by a vicious dog, ponders on his ageing body and, that which is "behind" him, present but ghosting him, are the memories of his late wife,

no longer
will she call, will she not,
and in walks too
there's a pitted path
for a head in a battered cap

"[K]ids at their games" is a memoir, a collection of tanka about his past, his heritage and history. In this minimalist tanka,

the way
the wind took
that kite
infinite
the length of spring

Goldstein brilliantly captures the joy of flying a kite. Elsewhere, as in "substitutions", although he has been celibate for years, he still enjoys his solitude, eating a pie in his favourite café and enjoying the safeness beneath his Japanese counterpane.

In "tanka gyrations," the poet tackles a recurring theme, that of his devotion to tanka. It is the sole thing which, through its production, publication and the joy it brings him, is a validation of his existence:

it's on paper
I have my other life,
the life
that has no causes to uphold,
no core to suck

To this poetic exploration of life, family and writing, Goldstein adds some fine tanka on writers, painters and literary characters, such as Van Gogh, Emily Dickinson, Henry James, Hamlet, Gatsby. The final poem in "staccato illusions" is this beautiful, evocative tanka about Anne Frank and his visit to the attic in which she survived for a period during WWII,

Anne Frank
how you scribbled
endured,
and now I tramp up these stairs
they hurried you down

Here, as elsewhere, fact and fiction are used skillfully to compare and contrast the themes of his life.

While the tanka in *This Tanka Whirl* fill the book with a rich tone and widen the emotional range, the poems are further enhanced through the author's final string, "this stumped self". In this sequence, the focus is on the poet's image of himself: his face, his "mirror-image" and his "coined-tossed" life. The final enigmatic poem,

at the end
of my white string
a soulmate came,
so close to the edge
I could not scissor it away

leaves us in little doubt that the poet is anticipating his death after a long life of writing and teaching. I feel that his soulmate is his dead wife whom he hopes will be there to meet and guide him into the afterlife.

These are tanka with which to study and reflect on the life and work of a great poet. Throughout, the tone and the details are sometimes raw and affecting, creating a dialogue with the reader about the poet and his life, rending it as the space of domesticity, work and love of his craft. This is a book which draws the reader back again and again into its richly suggestive poems.

Review: *All You Need Is Love,* Edited by Amelia Fielden

Reviewed by Patricia Prime

All You Need Is Love
Amelia Fielden, Editor
Australia
Ginninderra Press www.gininnderrapress.com.au
Pb. 62 pp
ISBN: 978-1-74027-918-5
Obtainable from Amelia Fielden at
anafielden@gmail.com for US $15 including
airmail postage.

In the title of this anthology of tanka, edited by Amelia Fielden, is subtext familiar possibly to many people from a particular time when they listened to the Beatles. So there is a theme which is not especially new, but each time in the telling, it is original and unique to each poet.

An anthology is a form that allows an editor to cast a wide imaginative net over a large group of poets and here are featured over 60 Australian poets. There is not the same constraint as with autobiography or memoir. In these tanka, the emotional landscape is navigated perhaps more creatively and perhaps more truthfully.

I read the anthology, the first time as a reader and writer of tanka, the second as a reviewer. Both times I was challenged by the editor's choice, to not only re-imagine what each poet is trying to convey, but to place their words into this re-imagining. In second reading, I will admit, I was more able to 'let go' of my own feelings and see clearly how these recollections, using family, friends, loved ones, pets and truth, is a device for laying out the foundations of the theme of love.

Whatever the setting, the tanka remain personal, and this touching accessibility, it seems to me, is a great poetic gift. As Lynette Arden's tanka illustrates love is also part of life that we devote to our pets,

I keep
living it over
late at night
after he stopped breathing
the softness of his fur

Belinda Broughton makes the character of her daughter and a young girl's all-too-human characteristic love of pretty things real,

around her neck
shells and hag stones—
my hippy daughter
with love in the spring
of her step

For Rhonda Byrne it's a forty-year friendship which gives her joy,

surprise!
a Valentine's Day card
in my mailbox
our forty-year friendship
turns a new page

Sylvia Florin's use of evocative language about India makes us dream about a trip to that exotic country,

her dark locks
uncoiling under moonlight
Ganga rushes by
. . . to a longed-for tryst
with the waiting plain

There is something impressionistic, colourful, inventive and modern about David Gilbey's diction in his tanka. His way with words is a vehicle to articulate the intricacies of a relationship,

her email keens
at the airport wifi lounge
where are you? come back—
he replies, stroking her neck,
internet kiss marks

Here are tanka that examine not just the bond between man and woman, parents and children, lovers and countries, but how a love of nature is ever present, as we see in Margaret L. Grace's tanka about her garden and the nest she finds blown down in a storm,

in my garden
intricately woven
softly lined
this small storm-blown nest . . .
anguished cries from above

There are also tanka that consider the role men play in the family dynamic. Tanka such as Simon Hanson's,

approaching
headlights in the mist
dip over the hill
raising my hopes
it might be you

and James Holcombe's fine poem about the beauty and pleasure of a personal relationship,

seeing in colours
radiant from a simple smile
ever since that first kiss
an angel on the earth
a friend to lie beside

Andrew Howe's tanka,

children's fingers
pollinate orchid to bean
vanilla . . .
taste of love
scent of sophistication

offsets the traditional perceptions of masculinity (strength, objectivity, inexpression) with an authentic portrayal of masculinity within family relationships.

Many of the tanka are concerned with how people connect and the intriguing interplay that results. The meaning of human existence is mediated through our feelings for each other,

what we believe and what we can achieve. Tension offers powerfully comparable and distinct explorations of the human and humanity. Sometimes the poetry-scapes of these tanka are family, sometimes strangers or places; often they are personal, often they are profound. Read them individually, but, given how much associative territory they examine, delving into them as a group might be the way to go.

Review: *Gusts No. 21* Edited by Kozue Uzawa

Reviewed by Patricia Prime

GUSTS
Kozue Uzawa, editor
Canada
Royal Printers: www.royalprinters.com
Pb. 32 pp
ISSN: 1715-3581
Subscription only: Canada $22 Canadian; US $28; International US$36 for two issues: spring/summer; fall/winter.

Gusts: Contemporary Tanka is the biannual publication of Tanka Canada. Membership includes two issues: spring/summer and autumn/winter. The journal is edited by Kozue Uzawa.

The contents of Issue 21 include 32 sections of tanka ranging through various themes including children, wildlife, ageing, health and writing. Each issue contains one to three tanka per poet. The tanka are beautifully presented in two columns of 12 poems per page: the large format giving plenty of white space between and around each tanka.

There are also four reviews in this issue: *The Sarashina Diary: a Woman's Life in Eleventh-Century Japan* by Sonja Arntzen and Itō Moriyuki, reviewed by Maxianne Berger; *Hedgerows: tanka pentaptychs* by Joy McCall, reviewed by Joanne

Morcom; *Treewhispers*, tanka by Giselle Maya, reviewed by Marjorie Buettner and *Faces I Might Wear*, tanka by Carol Purington, reviewed by Carole MacRury.

Tanka featured in this volume are by poets from USA, Canada, Australia, Germany, Romania, Japan, France, New Zealand, Australia, UK and South Africa. The recent work of these poets intersects, even nods in agreement, on common concerns. But although these writers may seem on the surface to be of a type—mainly women, previously published, some of them editors themselves or with published books of tanka—their absorbing difference of form and content burrows deeply into their various lives, countries, outlooks and interests.

The tanka are gathered into themes—with tangential thoughts expressed in plain language that nevertheless picks delicately over the subtlest, lightest, deepest concepts.

In John Quinnett's tanka he is an adult, a cheerful soul who ponders on what he remembers about his childhood:

> to the woods
> gathering mushrooms
> the child inside
> remembers the joy
> of hunting colored eggs

The conversational tone of Susan Diridoni's tanka is never banal but takes the reader into the depths of a relationship:

> our first meeting
> one look at your eyes, luminous
> endless green
> I couldn't stop dreaming
> of swimming in their depths

Residing at the centre of Joyce Wong's tanka is a soul-searching plea about a whispered letter:

> early spring—
> a whispered letter
> on my lips
> remains unsent,
> if only you knew

Place is almost always important to poets and Elena Calvo miraculously conjures up her grandparents' house:

> visiting
> my grandparent's country home
> in Puerto Rico
> the once stately stairway
> now leads to nowhere

The tanka array themselves over a broad spectrum of subjects, yet build intractably so that each poem unfolds something new and progresses the whole satisfactorily. Early advice in Kurt F. Svatek's 'the way home' (p.7) is offset by J. Zimmerman's 'Cooking lasagna' (p.8). And a wistful account in Maria Steyn's 'a murmur of doves' (p. 11) morphs into sounds in Jenny Ward Angyal's 'cold fog' (p. 13).

It is a world where everything is saying something secret to us—from different tanka we can select 'a curious thought now / you've been dead a year' (Mary Franklin), 'a jarring ring / after hours of waiting—' (Ken Slaughter), 'the day erupts into loud dissensions' (Beverley George), 'researchers claim / insomnia shrinks the brain' (Lucille Raizada) and 'she was coming in / as I was on my way out' (Neal Whitman).

While Dawn Bruce develops the notion of ageing and does it delicately and sensitively in her tanka:

> in mid April
> I become older
> than my mother . . .
> reflections ghosting
> in an antique mirror

Each tanka in *Gusts* is self-contained and, for this reason, the journal can be dipped into to provide momentary access to other worlds. Accessible, a pleasure to read, it which will attract readers who may or may not write tanka and this is a great achievement.

Review: *From the Middle Country:* The Third Tanka Collection by Noriko Tanaka

Reviewed by Patricia Prime

From the Middle Country
Noriko Tanaka
Amelia Fielden & Saeko Ogi, translators
Adelaide, Australia
Ginninderra Press, 2015
www.gininnderrapress.com.au
Pb. 62 pp
ISBN 978 1 74027 905 6
Obtainable from anafielden@gmail.com for $10 + postage.

The widely known and respected tanka poets Amelia Fielden and Saeko Ogi have, in *From the Middle Country*, translated the third collection of tanka by Noriko Tanaka. The book has an attractive cover design, and the tanka are published from one to five to a page. The tanka are divided into three sections: I. From the Ocean Country: Blue Times; II. From the Middle Country: Onogoro Island and III. From the Country of the Dead: The Sleeping River. The tanka are followed by an Afterword by Noriko Tanaka and a brief biography.

The book opens with a Foreword by Michael McClintock, in which he says: "Noriko Tanaka's *From the Middle Country*, her third collection, is a powerful, compelling and exciting new testament to the brilliance possible in the tanka form. Here again, in the hands of a master, the art of tanka demonstrates its ability to adapt and change, to sing the songs that are relevant to a new, more globally orientated, generation."

In the first section, "From the Ocean Country: Blue Times" one discovers many delights and makes new discoveries, and I feel that readers of Tanaka's collection will find and discover new favourites for themselves, like the following tanka:

transparent bodies
of cuttlefish rising
higher and higher—
in the ocean, the blue
of another world

"Songs at the Bottom of the Sea" is an amusing and varied collection of tanka on the theme of the sea. Here we can read about salamanders, crabs, minnows, sea-otters, seals and a variety of sea life, such as this poem about moon jellies:

moon jellies,
oh, how chilly must be
the bottom of the water—
when I
think of you

But this cluster of tanka ends on a note of personal gravity:

this town has sunk
into the evening gloom—
I am
like a black fish
swimming along

"Falling into the Sea" begins with an amusing tanka about rain falling from the sky:

high in the sky
sounds of a sewing machine
treadling—
rain, you are
a really hard worker

In the second section, "From the Middle Country: Onogoro Island", the subjects range from stirring stew, the blue train, classroom windows, the water's surface, cicadas and writing or perhaps translating tanka:

with a single particle
as clue, I'm investigating
several thousand tanka
on this night
of early summer rain

"The Sea of Trees" covers another range of topics without ever losing the theme of nature. Tanaka also has a way with humour that holds a subtle touch of poignancy, but still tempts the reader to empathise with her, as in this tanka where she writes about herself in ironic tones,

having raised
this plump body of mine
swollen with fluid,
I was researching
the kanji character for 'moon'

"Fireflies" is more playful, less poignant, only now and again hinting at the shadows beneath her words,

I dream of
raw-green fleabane weeds
sprouting,
and my whole body
turning into a forest

In "The Tree of Forbidden Fruit," we learn more about Tanaka and her sense of fun,

in a lecture
at the beginning of autumn
I heard the theory
that the 'forbidden fruit' tree
referred to tomatoes

The third section, "From the Country of the Dead: The Sleeping River", hints at the darkness that lies beneath life. The surface meaning is sustained by what lies beneath, as in this tanka about a dream,

in a dream
when I was crying out
to be saved,
only the stardust
looked beautiful

"Strange Tales from the World of Spirits" concentrates on the world of spirits and provides a recognisable theme in which the inexpressible finds form. These vivid evocations of strange tales, murder, relationships, monsters and misunderstandings are very moving, as in this memory of the poet's father,

beyond the dripping
of the rain
are low clouds—
my deceased father's fingers
flick the abacus

"A Cloud on a Winter's Day" experiments across a wide range of subjects: a cloud, the winter sky, the moon, a dream, a crowded carriage and the lovely tanka about hearing a knock on the door,

the spring mountain
is fast asleep, when
I hear the sound
of knocking on the door
to the next room

Foremost in the poet's mind in "The Solar Eclipse" is her positive, humorous view of herself,

when I come up
onto the roof to see
the solar eclipse,
the wind there whispers
'I don't need you'

In "A Bird on the Mountain Top", she juxtaposes the dot made by her pen to the tiny insect crawling across the page,

tinier than the dot
made by my pen nib,
is the insect
walking across
the top of my notebook

"Rayleigh Scattering" contains five tanka about the sky, among other subjects, she writes about the common theme of love:

wanting only
to hear him say the words
'I love you',
I was gazing up
at the blue of the winter sky

In "Snowy Days" Tanaka expresses feelings for a young homosexual, a boy she doesn't recognise, in a dream and the face of a woman typing. But in the following tanka she tells a rueful story about a man laughing at someone's misfortune,

he was a young man
laughing as he told
the story
of a woman who
was deceived and died

In "Blossoms" the theme of the tanka are flowers, a cat, pears, white roses and a sinful apple. Deception again features in the following tanka,

as I deceive myself
over and over again,
the aroma
of a sinful apple
spreads through my mouth

The tanka in "Myths and Legends of the Middle Country" focus on myths such as the following,

grass grows away
and turns into fireflies:
the legend
I remembered
one rainy night

"The Dugong's Bones" contains five tanka: one about the dugong and another on the shadowless moving creatures in a village,

one could call this
a village with downcast eyes—
rain is falling
and there are not even shadows
from moving creatures

"From the Country of Forests: Tarō's Condolence Call" comes the lovely tanka,

warming his flute
in his bosom, Tarō
went swaying along
in the steam train
to make a condolence call

"From the Old Country: Earth Spiders" contains tanka about the poet's deceased parents and her return to her ancestral land, Yamoto. This beautiful tanka is a lyrical paean for her parents,

the silent stillness
of mountains and swirling clouds—
autumn has come
to that hill where
my parents now sleep

The tanka in "I Am Not Crying" complete the sections, where we see the poet on a day of loneliness contemplating her parents,

a day when loneliness
wells up like water
in a salt jar—
the island is my father,
the ocean is my mother

Above all, in writing on all these themes and subjects, there are the charm, style, and the experiences of the poet. She has an engaging poise when she writes of serious topics; and an amusing sense of humour when writing about less serious ones. Everything is seen with a quality of lightness that doesn't diminish the solemnity of the subjects. Tanaka is a fine craftswoman of tanka, and her abilities are sustained throughout the collection. The choice of language is clear and simple, with rhythm and sound balancing the poems. There is no doubt that anyone wanting to read or study tanka would do well to study the craft of this elegant poet.

ANNOUNCEMENTS

Atlas Poetica will publish short announcements in any language up to 300 words in length on a space available basis. Announcements may be edited for brevity, clarity, grammar, or any other reason. Send announcements in the body of an email to: AtlasPoetica@gmail.com—do not send attachments.

Preface to *Fire Pearls 2* Added to *Atlas Poetica* Resource Page

Keibooks has posted the Preface to *Fire Pearls 2 : Short Masterpieces of Love and Passion* edited by M. Kei online at http://atlaspoetica.org/?page_id=1419.

In the Preface, M. Kei gives a history of tanka sequences in English and discusses terminology and concepts essential for understanding sequences as a poet or a reader.

The Preface appears in the 'Resources' section where AtlasPoetica.org publishes articles and reference material of use to readers, writers, and editors of tanka.

*　*　*

Special Feature 'Myths and the Creative Imagination' Published by Atlas Poetica

*Atlas Poetica : A Journal of World Tank*a announces the publication of a new special feature, 'Myths and the Creative Imagination' edited by Sonam Chhoki. "Twenty-five poets from around the world attest to the power of myths to open up the world of imagination. Some delve into the rich symbolism, others draw out the resonance that particular myths have for them, and still others interpret the theme of this special feature to explore their own personal myths."—from the editor.

Visit http://atlaspoetica.org/?page_id=1382 to read for free.

Sample Poems:

how can I fault
the curious Pandora
for opening the jar—
I thought my face cream too
promised eternal youth

Margaret Chula, Portland, Oregon, USA

an ant
on this pilgrim path . . .
oh teach me, Santiago
the size of today
the strength of now

Carole Harrison, Jamberoo, Australia

from a ball of flesh
Queen Gandhara brings forth
her Kaurava clan . . .
science celebrates Louise Brown,
the first test-tube baby

Pravat Kumar Padhy, Odisha, India

the humming of the clock
fading now to silence
by your bedside
half a world away
a banshee prepares to sing

John Tehan, Cape Cod, Massachusetts, USA

Contributors: Jenny Ward Angyal, an'ya, Marjorie Buettner, Margaret Chula, Tish Davis, Sanford Goldstein, Autumn Noelle Hall, Carole Harrison, Elizabeth Howard, Marilyn Humbert, Gerry Jacobson, Chen-ou Liu, Gregory Longenecker, Vasile Maldovan, Joy McCall, Mike Montreuil, Pravat Kumar Padhy, Patricia Prime, Aruna Rao, Miriam Sagan, Debbie Strange, John Tehan, Laura Williams, Kath Abela Wilson, Ali Znaidi.

Announcing
This Tanka Whirl, 2nd Edition, by Sanford Goldstein

"Reading Goldstein's *This Tanka Whirl* the image of the double helix springs to mind: a spiral stairway of two strands inter-twined, neither of which can exist without the other. A master of the form, Goldstein writes with honesty and humility; his is an everyday world, but it is not without its thrills and spills, joy and anguish. He rages against the tameness of his tanka, invoking the music of inner worlds that have 'gone berserk'; here, too, he would be Ishmael, driven by his own white whale.

Eight decades and he can no more set down his tanka brush, 'this cascade of me! and my! and mine!' than this dervish earth can bow out of the cosmic dance. This is a poet who sits, pen in hand, in the eye of the storm, drawing ink from Van Gogh's swirling petals, Mokichi's yellow tears, Gatsby's glitter. . .

This is a poet who would have Hamlet tread the boards of his own short song, only to look the Prince squarely in the eye and exclaim: '. . . I feel even tanka / can scale the spectacular'. In your hands, Mr Goldstein, indeed, it can."—Claire Everett, Founder and Editor of *Skylark, A Tanka Journal*

This Tanka Whirl
(second edition)
by Sanford Goldstein
with an introduction by M. Kei
ISBN-13: 978-1508943525
Perfect bound; 68 pages; 6 x 9 inches
$8.00 plus postage.

Winfred Press
374 Wilson Hill Road
Colrain, MA 01340
<winfred@crocker.co>

Note: As all shipments will be made through the Amazon online Book Store your order will arrive sooner if ordered directly from Amazon.com.

2015 TSA Members' Anthology

The Tanka Society of America is pleased to announce the publication of a members' anthology in the fall of 2015. This year's anthology will be edited by Claire Everett, a widely known tanka poet and editor of *Skylark Tanka Journal*. David Rice, TSA's *Ribbons* editor, will do the design and production. We're very excited about this anthology, which will complete a year of events celebrating TSA's fifteenth anniversary.

—Margaret Chula, TSA president and anthology liaison

Submission Guidelines

Submit: Send five to ten unpublished tanka. TSA members who send at least five submissions will be guaranteed the selection of at least one tanka for the anthology. Socially published poems (Twitter, Facebook, author blogs) are eligible for submission as long as they are indicated as such.

Eligibility: Open to poets who are current (2015) members of the Tanka Society of America or those who join within the submission period. If you're not a current member, please join or renew today.

Submission period: September 1–30, 2015.

Submit to: The editor, Claire Everett at inkstonemoon@gmail.com, with the subject line of "TSA Submission—Your Name." Please include your complete name (as you would like it to appear in the anthology) and your address with your submission. Automated acknowledgements of receipt will be sent to contributors. If you don't receive one, please contact Claire Everett.

Publication date: Copies will be available for purchase on Lulu.com ($10 + S&H) in the late fall.

Register for Tanka Sunday: October 18, 2015

The Tanka Society of America is pleased to announce its third conference, Tanka Sunday 2015, to be held on October 18, 2015 (the last day of the Haiku North America conference) at the Desmond Hotel in Albany, New York. We've decided to make the event FREE to everyone, members and nonmembers alike. Complete Information about registration, the schedule, bookfair, and our keynote speaker, Amy Vladeck Heinrich, is now online at http://www.tankasocietyofamerica.org/tanka-sunday-2015.

Other confirmed presenters include Pamela A. Babusci, Tom Clausen, Marilyn Hazelton, Mariko Kitakubo, and David Terelinck. If you have questions, contact Tanka Sunday organizers Michael Dylan Welch (WelchM@aol.com) or Kathabela Wilson (poetsonsite@gmail.com). We hope you can join us for this event amid the autumn colors of upstate New York! Check out the website for all the details, and please register as soon as you can.

Keibooks Announces *flowers to the torch : American Tanka Prose* by Peter Fiore

In *flowers to the torch* Peter Fiore revitalizes the tanka prose tradition by turning it on its head. Most of these poems are divided into five sections, some have a poem as a section, some have two. Some have none. But throughout Fiore maintains the feel of tanka—the delicacy of the moment, a heightened sense of language, and the importance of five which links it all to one of the oldest known poetic forms. Five fingers on each hand, five toes, and the five senses—our most primal ways of knowing the world.

"At last, and worth waiting for. Peter Fiore's own half century, a lifetime discipline of appetite and mystery, escape and dismay. Poems . . . full of broken hearts, whirling snow and flight." And finally—where we all end up, out of escapes—he still manages to find an angel."—Art Beck, poet, and translator of *Luxorius Opera Omnia, a Duet for Sitar and Trombone*

flowers to the torch : American Tanka Prose
by peter fiore
Edited by M. Kei
ISBN-13: 978-1507577356 (Print) 86 pp
$12.00 USD / £8.00 GBP / €11.00 EUR
$5.00 USD (Kindle)

Purchase in print at: https://www.createspace.com/5260725
Also available in print and ebook at Amazon.com and other online retailers.

Publications by Keibooks

Atlas Poetica : A Journal of Poetry of Place in Contemporary Tanka

Collections Edited by M. Kei

Warp and Weft, Tanka Threads, by Debbie Strange (forthcoming)

flowers to the torch : American Tanka Prose, by peter fiore

rising mist, fieldstones, by Joy McCall

Hedgerows, Tanka Pentaptychs, by Joy McCall

circling smoke, scattered bones, by Joy McCall

Tanka Left Behind : Tanka from the Notebooks of Sanford Goldstein, by Sanford Goldstein

This Short Life, Minimalist Tanka, by Sanford Goldstein

Anthologies Edited by M. Kei

Bright Stars, An Organic Tanka Anthology (Vols. 1–7)

Take Five : Best Contemporary Tanka (Vol. 4)

M. Kei's Poetry Collections

January, A Tanka Diary

Slow Motion : The Log of a Chesapeake Bay Skipjack
tanka and short forms

Heron Sea : Short Poems of the Chesapeake Bay
tanka and short forms

M. Kei's Novels

Pirates of the Narrow Seas 1 : The Sallee Rovers
Pirates of the Narrow Seas 2 : Men of Honor
Pirates of the Narrow Seas 3 : Iron Men
Pirates of the Narrow Seas 4 : Heart of Oak

Man in the Crescent Moon : A Pirates of the Narrow Seas Adventure
The Sea Leopard : A Pirates of the Narrow Seas Adventure

Fire Dragon

Made in the USA
Lexington, KY
23 August 2015